# Making
# Vegetables
## Volume 1
### By Shoshanna Easling

*J* grew up on a farm in the middle of an Amish community. I know you are wondering—no, I am not Amish. My parents were artists and ministered to the service men and women in the Memphis, Tennessee, area. When I was three, my parents decided they wanted to raise us five kids in the country. So we, the Pearl family, moved to a 100-acre, beautiful farm that bordered Cane Creek. There we were in paradise—hunting, fishing, camping, canoeing, tubing, gardening, and preserving our harvest. Life was good! Twenty-six years later all five of us children are happily married and still living life to the fullest. Nine years ago I married James Easling. We are best friends and, well, we like each other! We have Jeremiah James (seven years old) and Penelope Jane (two years old). We own the Bulk Herb Store and work it together with our ten employees. We are going beyond what we know and are researching and learning so we can teach our children. Gardening is a delight in our lives. We are healthy and our food is delicious!

*James, Shoshanna, Jeremiah (7 years old), and Penelope (2 years old) Easling*

First Edition April 2013
ISBN-10: 1937478025
ISBN-13: 978-1937478025

MAKING VEGETABLES

Editor in Chief: Shoshanna Easling

Design & Layout: Audrey Madill

Photography: Laura Newman Photography
Lauren Brandt
Jeremiah James Easling
Shoshanna Easling
Becky Schrock

Illustrations: Benjamin Aprile
James Easling

To the Love of My Life, James Easling

I dedicate this series to you, James Easling! I want to thank you for letting me shine. You encourage me and push me to be a better person. You have given me wings to fly and I soar. I am able to write books and help people because we are united as one, and I am stronger because of you. To God be the glory; great things he has done. God has given me you! I LOVE YOU!

The queen of your heart,
Shoshanna Easling

# Contents

# Introduction

Traditionally grown foods are full of chemicals, pesticides, sprays, additives, and preservatives. We think we are keeping ourselves healthy by eating vegetables, but if we only knew what was on and in them, we would think again. Organic vegetables are cleaner and better for your body.

## Better Than Organic?

Yes! You can have better than organic vegetables. Just because something is organic does not mean that it is full of vitamins, minerals, and nutrients. Some organic vegetables and fruits are grown in nothing but sand like the traditionally grown ones. The problem is that sand does not provide the nutrients that are needed to grow nutritional vegetables or fruits.

## Dying from Malnutrition

As a country, we are overeating but the nutritional value is not there. We are a fat nation dying from malnutrition. Without the right nutrients, our bodies are susceptible to disease and cannot repair themselves as they were designed to do.

Barry Estabrook writes in his book *Tomatoland*, "According to analyses conducted by the U.S. Department of Agriculture, 100 grams of fresh tomato today has 30 percent less vitamin C, 30 percent less thiamin, 19 percent less niacin, and 62 percent less calcium than it did in the 1960s. But the modern tomato does shame its 1960s counterpart in one area: It contains 14 times as much sodium."

What we eat matters, and how we grow it matters even more. It's time to put our knowledge into practice . . . for our health and for our children's.

Jeremiah James is our wonderful little gardener! He is holding an eggplant that he picked.

# The Greenhouse

*G*reenhouses are so much fun! Fresh veggies all winter long really spoil you. I grew up where everyone had a greenhouse. Little did I know using a greenhouse would become a dying art and a great loss to the coming generation. Let's bring them back!

# Greenhouse Basics

For instructions on building different types of greenhouses, see pages 125-147.

## Heat and Light

You can heat your greenhouse with a conventional heater or woodstove. We built ours into the hillside facing south for light and heat. Having it partially in the ground with the south side open to the sun helps it to naturally heat itself. If it gets below freezing for a number of days, I stick a heater in it on low for the duration of the cold spell.

## Seedling Heat Mats

A heat mat is nice for seed starting in a cooler area; it's like a low-heat greenhouse. It is a thin pad that plugs in and heats on a low temperature. It is made to set your trays on to start seeds or grow plants in cool weather. Heat mats can be purchased online. See Resources (page 277).

## Pollination

Pollination makes your flowers produce fruit. It is an essential part of fruit production. It is cold outside in February, but there are bees still out there pollinating in my greenhouse. I leave the door open whenever it is not freezing outside, and the bees come to pollinate my flowers.

## Ventilation

Ventilation is very important in a greenhouse. The sun can warm it up very quickly and fry your plants, even if it is chilly outside. Open your greenhouse door if it is warming up too much, or install temperature-activated vent fans.

Penelope Jane's
favorite person is my
"Papa Pearl".

# CD Greenhouse

I crack up every time I see my dad's greenhouse. Is it a work of art or a hillbilly's dream?

I am not sure, but I remember when he built it. About ten years ago, he dug a hole in the south-facing hillside and laid blocks. Having it mostly underground allows him to grow things all winter without heating it. Because it is partially underground, Dad wanted to increase his available light, which helps the plants grow and boosts the heat in the greenhouse. He did not have the money to spend on a lot of mirrors, but he had a box of a few thousand old CDs that did not have a place, and yes, he used them all. There was so much light bouncing around! It really did work!

So use what you have. Be creative. We were poor growing up but always had lots of fresh veggies. Old windows, doors, and CDs can be the makings of a great greenhouse. It might not always look pretty, but it can grow some pretty stuff!

# Greenhouse *Alternatives*

## Warm, Sunlit Window >>

You do not need a greenhouse to start your seeds. You can grow them in any sunlit window. South windows tend to work best. My mom always had seeds starting in her kitchen window.

## Grow Lights

Many people who do not have a feasible window use a grow light. Grow lights are not expensive and they work really well. They can even be used to grow things in your basement! They look just like normal florescent shop lights, but they give off the light your plants need to grow. You can use them to start seeds or to sustain plants through the winter. Make sure you get a "cool white" florescent light. Hang lights 4–6 inches above the plants. As they grow, raise lights to maintain proper distance. Grow lights can be purchased at Lowe's. See Resouces (page 280) for other places to find grow lights.

## Hot Box

Building a hot box is an easy way to have fresh veggies in the cold weather. Just dig a hole, build a box frame, add green manure and soil, and top with a window, door, or any clear cover. You have a hot box! Basically it is an underground, self-heating greenhouse. It is easy to build and does not take a lot of room. Check out how to build it in Projects on pages 120-123.

## Early Crops

There are many cool-weather crops that are great for unheated or low-heat winter beds. In Tennessee, I have many crops growing long into the winter in my hot box, raised beds, greenhouse, and even in my garden with row covers. Check out these in Projects (pages 120-147).

## Covering Plants

Covering plants for growing is not that difficult. You can use recycled bottles, cups, boxes, plastic, sheets, blankets, straw, garden fleece, or anything else you have on hand.

# Seed Spitting

I grew up in paradise, a little Amish community called Cane Creek. Middle Tennessee is full of rolling hills and spring water. Where I lived was one of the prettiest places on earth. My parents were artists, evangelists, and down-to-earth great parents. We had moved from Memphis to this little spot when I was three years old. We were not Amish, but we lived off the land and learned from their simple lifestyle. We grew and preserved all of our food. My dad and my brothers hunted game for our meat. One of my favorite things about living in the community was the creek the community is named for.

*"Summer always meant lots of watermelons, tomatoes, and cantaloupe. That meant delicious food fights! Seed spitting was a sport."*

Cane Creek borders a good part of Dad's property. Every summer afternoon my sisters and I would go down to the creek. We would swim in the cool water, get cold, and then lie in the sun on the hot rocks of the gravel bar. I can still feel the hot rocks with the sun on my back, and remember the taste of watermelon in my mouth. We would have races going under water and swimming like mermaids. We swung on the rope and laughed until it hurt, every day. Or, at least, Shalom and I did. Rebekah would read her books and move around like she was the queen of England. She was nine and a half years older, and I thought she, with all her beauty, could be the queen of England. Those were some of the best days of my life.

Summer always meant lots of watermelons, tomatoes, and cantaloupe. That meant delicious food fights! Seed spitting was a sport. The gravel bar always had little watermelon plants springing up from the seeds we left behind. That is when I learned that seeds are not real fussy; they WANT to grow. You can eat a watermelon, spit the seeds, and get a plant—in a gravel bar, no less. Our compost pile of discarded veggies always had 25 little tomato plants growing around it. This year I was reminded of it again when I went over to my mom and dad's house and there were a dozen volunteer tomato plants loaded with sweet little tomatoes. Life is good!

Seed
Starte

A lot of plants benefit from being started indoors (in a greenhouse, near a sunny window, or with grow lights) to get an early start. Other plants do better planted directly in the garden.

## What You Need for Seed Starting

The basic seed-starting method is to sprinkle or sow seeds in shallow containers to germinate, and then transplant into individual cells/pots. The plants will then grow in those pots until they are big enough for the garden. This method will take your seedlings through three different stages. (There are a few plants that do not like to be transplanted; these exceptions will be mentioned later.)

The first stage is the germination stage, which is the period from when you plant your seed until it sprouts and emerges from the soil. Stage two is the time after germination until the seedlings are ready to be transplanted into individual cells/pots. Stage three is transplanting and growing your seedling in its own cell/pot until it is ready for the garden. Now, lets figure out what kind of containers you will need.

Jeremiah James bought some pumpkin seeds!

# Trays

For sprinkling seeds, you can use anything that is non-metal and about 2 or 3 inches deep. Tupperware, plastic storage containers, or cardboard boxes cut down to several inches deep are just a few containers that work well. Make sure your trays have drainage holes. If they do not, you can drill 5 to 10 holes in the bottom, depending on how big they are. If trays don't have good drainage, seeds can easily get too wet, which causes them to rot.

Ideal containers for transplanting seedlings will vary with different plants. It also depends on how long you will be growing them in the pot. Some of my favorites are 1203 and 1204 cell trays (1203 means there are 12 packs in a tray, with 3 cells in each pack). 1204 cell trays work great for most vegetables if

*Drilling Holes:*

you plant them in the garden at the optimum size. I use 1203s for things like squash and pumpkins and anything else I want to give a little more room to grow. Herbs are plants that like a little bigger pot, usually a 4-inch one. Tomatoes can quickly outgrow their pots, too, if they don't get planted right away. You may want to plant them in bigger pots as well.

You can buy cell trays and other pots at greenhouse supply stores (see Resources). You can also use foam coffee cups, egg cartons, rolled up newspapers, or any other repurposed container you can think of!

# Soil

Good potting soil is light and fluffy and usually contains sphagnum peat moss, vermiculite, and/or perlite. The main ingredient is usually peat moss, although some organic mixes have coconut coir fiber instead of peat, which works great as well. Peat moss is just moss. It is a stable, organic ingredient that holds a lot of water and air. Vermiculite and perlite are natural mineral substances that help make the potting soil lightweight and porous, holding water and nutrients that are released over time.

It is best to use a soilless mix (meaning there is no garden soil or topsoil in the mix). Garden soil will be too heavy and too compact for good air circulation and is likely to carry disease organisms that cause root-rot and damping-off diseases in seedlings.

You do not have to buy a mix that is labeled "germinating mix" to start your seeds. Germinating mix is very fine (and also more expensive) and will not be suitable for growing plants long-term. You can just buy regular potting soil, and if it is rather coarse, you can sift it through a screen. This will make it easier for fine seeds to germinate.

You should be able to find a green-

house/produce grower supply store in your area. That will be the best place to get good potting soil and other supplies. Garden centers like Lowe's or Home Depot also carry organic potting soil, but they tend to have the heavier, compost-based mixes. You can also get greenhouse supplies on the Internet (see Resources).

## Organic or Not

You do not have to use organic potting soil. If you are having a hard time finding a nice fluffy potting soil, you can use a non-organic one. Most potting soils have a base of all-natural ingredients, but they have wetting agents and inorganic jump-start fertilizers added. By the time the seedling is ready to plant, a lot of the wetting agents and fertilizers will have been watered out of it. I still prefer going organic all the way, but you can use what you have even if it is not organic.

## Make Your Own Potting Soil

You can also make your own potting soil. A mixture of peat moss, some perlite, and/or vermiculite plus organic fertilizers makes a great potting soil. Compost tea will work as an organic wetting agent.

Jeremiah James is my little photographer.

*Worm castings (left), vermiculite (top center), perlite (center), peat moss (right)*

# Potting Soil

Good, organic potting soil is not always easy to find. Here is a potting soil recipe that you can make.

- 4 parts sphagnum peat moss
- 2 parts worm castings
- 1½ parts perlite
- 1 part vermiculite.

For more nutrients, add ¼ cup of balanced all-purpose fertilizer (page 177-178) to every gallon of finished potting soil. Spray with compost tea, or mix in a little water to dampen it before putting it into trays/pots. The peat moss will repel water at first until it is moistened through.

# Seeds

It all starts with a seed, but not all seeds are equal. There are some things you need to know before buying seeds. Check out pages 187-191 and 204-208 to learn the difference between heirloom, open-pollinated, hybrid, and GMO seeds. See Resources (pages 277-281) for good places to buy heirloom seeds.

Heirloom Expo
Seed Art

# Greenhouse Fertilizers

Plant-tone All-Purpose Organic Fertilizer (Espoma brand), liquid fish organic fertilizer, and compost tea are a few great ways to feed your seedlings. Plant-tone (available at Lowe's) is a granular fertilizer that you mix into your potting soil. Liquid fish and compost tea can be applied throughout the growing period of your seedlings.

Most people don't use fertilizer to start seeds but wait until plants get a little older. I have found that seeds don't need many nutrients to germinate, but they benefit from a little. A general rule is to cut fertilizer rates in half for germination and young seedlings. I like to mix Plant-tone (at one-half suggested rates) into my potting soil before I plant seeds.

Then, I water them gently with a liquid fish solution. Use the fertilizers at one-half rates until seedlings are ready to transplant. Liquid fish can be applied once a week.

## About Liquid Fish

Liquid fish is made out of fish carcasses. There are two kinds of liquid fish on the market: Neptune's Harvest Organic Liquid Fish, and one that is referred to as fish emulsion. The difference is that Neptune's Harvest fish fertilizer is made by a cold process that retains all the oils, vitamins, enzymes, and amino acids in the finished product. Fish emulsion removes the oils and uses a heated process that destroys the vitamins, enzymes, and amino acids. The finished product is a little higher in nitrogen and feeds the plants faster, but it doesn't have all the enzymes that benefit your soil.

## Compost Tea

Compost tea is made by brewing compost into a tea—by taking a small amount of compost and mixing it in water. Then it is aerated at the perfect temperature so the good microbial life can multiply rapidly. Then you spray it on the plants to give them amazing nutrients. It also is a great way to help protect them from pests and disease. Compost tea is the extra boost that every plant loves! A simple, easy way to make it is to buy a compost tea brewing mix that is specially formulated for making compost tea. (See Resources - pages 277-278). Or you can use your own compost - check out *Making Vegetables Volume 3* for more information on compost and how to make it.

## How to Make a Compost Tea Brewer

Materials you will need: (most can be purchased at a pet suppy store.)

5-gallon bucket

Aquarium hose (about 10 feet will be enough)

(2) tee connectors

(2) 1-inch air stones

(2) 5-inch air stones

(1) aquarium pump

(2) paint strainer bags (optional)

*1.* Cut two pieces of aquarium hose, each 2 to 3 feet long.

>>

2. Connect them to the two air outlets on the aquarium pump.

3. Attach a tee connector to the opposite end of each hose.

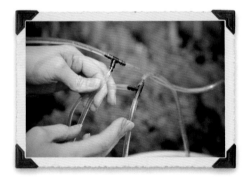

4. Cut four 6-inch pieces of hose, and attach to each end of the tee connectors.

5. Attach the two 5-inch air stones to one hose, and the 1-inch stones to the other.

6. Place air pump on a dry spot, higher than the tea brewer.

7. Place hoses in the bucket, putting stones on opposite sides of each other for even aeration.

8. Voila! Your brewer is ready to plug in and brew!

**Tip:** Many large organic growers use compost tea. Using high-quality compost, they will mix their compost and water, strain and spray immediately, skipping the brewing process to save time. This works too, but I still prefer it brewed.

## Brew Your Tea

The amount of compost you use will vary with different mixes. If you purchased a tea brewing mix, follow package instructions. If you are using plain compost or humus, then start with about 1 cup per 5 gallons of brew. Most bagged compost you buy at the store has been sterilized which kills all the living microbes that make compost tea. You will know your compost is alive if it builds up bubbles.

*1.* Put about 2–3 gallons of water in your tea brewer (you will need room for the bubbles).

*2.* Add compost or brewing mix and stir into the water. I like to add worm castings or other organic fertilizer for more nutrients. A good amount to start with is ½ cup. It doesn't take much!

*3.* Plug in and brew! Ideal temperature for brewing is 70°F. (See Tips.) After 8 to 12 hours you should be able to tell whether it is alive and bubbling. With really great compost bubbles can even come up over the rim of the bucket. Adjust the amount of compost accordingly, or if it doesn't bubble at all, use different compost.

*4.* After 24 hours of brewing, strain into another 5 gallon bucket using a piece of muslin or old cloth. Add water to make 5 gallons.

5. Apply immediately while microbes are still alive. Spray all over plants, and drench roots.

## Tips

You can also brew a concentrated batch using double or triple compost, and then dilute it after brewing.

Another method is to put your compost into a burlap or paint strainer bag. Lay a stick across the brewer and tie the bag to the stick so that the compost is just immersed in the water. Put the 1-inch air stones right in the bag. Check out video for demo.

Brewing at temperatures below 70° can also keep tea from building up bubbles, as it may not be warm enough to activate the microbes. Check to see if your temperature was right before switching compost.

## Notes

You will need a good backpack sprayer for gardening. Find one at Lowe's or greenhouse supply stores. Solo is a good brand.

If you are using a sprayer, you will still need to strain through a piece of muslin or an old sheet to keep the sprayer from clogging.

Oh, my word! Now I know where the Cinderella pumpkin story came from. We were at The National Heirloom Expo in Santa Rosa, California, and saw some of the biggest pumpkins in the world. These pumpkin growers use compost tea and humus like it is water. There were many pumpkins over a thousand pounds.

Mama watering the garden with Jeremiah and Penelope in it.

# Watering

You will need a gentle watering system that will not wash out your newly planted seeds. You can use a spray bottle, backpack sprayer, Wonder Waterer wand on a hose, or your kitchen spray faucet with low pressure.

(The Wonder Waterer is a must if you are growing a lot of seedlings. It is very gentle and can also water a lot in a short time. Find one online, or see Resources - page 278.)

The best water for plants is rainwater. It is easy to catch a barrel of rainwater for your plants. If that is not an option, you can use tap water, but see page 195 to learn more about tap water and what it can do to your plants.

Seed
Starting

# Stage 1:
## Starting Your Seeds

Now that you have pots, soil, seeds, fertilizer, and water, you are ready to get your fingers dirty and plant some seeds!

The following are two different ways to start seeds indoors.

### Method A

This method involves sprinkling seeds in shallow containers and then transplanting them into individual cells/pots after seedlings have two true leaves. This is the best way to start most seeds.

*1.* Put 1–2 inches of potting soil in tray/container.

*2.* Sprinkle seeds on top, not too thick.

*3.* Cover with about ¼-inch of soil for larger seed, while barely covering very fine seed.

*4.* Do not forget to label!

*5.* Water very gently with liquid fish solution or compost tea until soil is thoroughly moistened but not waterlogged.

*6.* Cover seed trays with plastic or put inside a plastic bag to retain moisture.

Place seeds in a warm spot – on top of your fridge, above a heater – wherever you can find a spot that is about 70–80°. DO NOT place in direct sunlight when covered with plastic.

*7.* Check on them at least once a day. If soil gets dry, water again. As soon as you see the first sprouts pushing up, remove the plastic and place in direct sunlight with temperature of about 65–70°.

## Method B

This method is to plant single seeds in individual pots. This is the best way to start large seeds like melons, pumpkins, squash, cucumbers, and other plants that do not like to be pulled apart and transplanted.

*1.* Fill cell trays/pots with potting soil.

*2.* Lay seed on top in middle of pot. (If you have old seed, or germination rate on seed packet is low, plant two seeds per pot.)

*3.* Press seed down 1 inch into potting soil and cover hole.

*4.* Follow steps 4 through 8 from method A.

Note

The temperatures mentioned on previous page are averages and are not specific for every vegetable. Most seedlings will do fine at those temperatures, but all seeds do not have the same preferences. See pages 50-54 for details on each vegetable.

## Tip for Hard-to-Start Seeds

Some seeds—like celery and parsley, and seeds that have a tough shell—can be hard to germinate. Soaking seeds in water will help them germinate faster.

1. Place them in a cup or bowl and cover with plenty of water. Let soak from 2 to 24 hours, depending on the variety.

2. Strain out the water and pour seeds on coffee filter. Let dry for about 10 minutes.

3. Plant immediately. Do not let seeds dry out completely before planting.

## Other Things to Know

You want to plant two to three times as many seeds as you need, since some might not germinate. Then you can pick out the healthiest ones to transplant.

Seeds love bottom heat to germinate (heat from the bottom). If needed, place seed trays on electric heat mats (see page 10) to increase the temperature by 10–20°.

Covering seed trays or containers with plastic helps to keep the warm air and moisture in. This really makes a big difference in the success of the germination process. You will need to keep them out of the sunlight, or the plastic will trap the sun's heat and cook your seeds. Seeds do not need light to germinate; in fact, they do better germinating in the dark. BUT they will need direct sunlight immediately after sprouting or they will grow thin, weak stems.

# Troubleshooting

*Just think about it!*

Last week a friend wrote and asked me if her plants were supposed to be 4 inches tall with only 2 little leaves on them. No, they are not! I think many people get discouraged planting their own seeds because they don't know what has gone wrong with their plants. Here are the answers to common troubleshooting questions.

### Are they too cold?

Temperatures below 60° for long periods of time can keep seeds from sprouting. It is best to keep temperature at a consistent range.

### Are they too wet?

If the soil is constantly soggy, seeds may rot, especially when temperatures are cold as well. If you think you watered too much, remove the plastic so it can dry out faster. Also, wet soil will not be as much of a problem if you keep it warm.

### Are they too dry?

If soil dries out completely, seeds will also dry out. Allowing seeds to dry out after they have been hydrated once may keep them from germinating.

### Are you using old seed?

Check your seed packet to see if seed is still viable. The older the seed gets, the lower the germination rate will be.

# Stage 2:
## Growing Seedlings

It is important to get your seeds in sunlight as soon as they start poking out through the soil. Keep them in germination temperatures until they are all up. Keep a close eye on them because as soon as they have all emerged they are ready to start building their strength by being exposed to the elements. Cooler weather, (just not below 40°) and some wind will help them grow properly. This will make them strong and healthy. Cold-sensitive plants like peppers, eggplant, basil, etc. are usually fine to keep indoors until they are bigger. Check out pages 55-57 to see which vegetables like it cool and which like it hot.

### Greenhouse

A greenhouse will provide the best light for your seedlings, but sometimes it is a challenge to keep it warm enough for germination, especially during the night. Heat mats come in handy for this problem.

You also need to keep a close eye on it in the daytime. If the sun is shining, it can easily get too hot. As soon as my seedlings are up, I like to open the door to my greenhouse during the day. If it is a colder day I will just barely open it, or if it is really cold and cloudy, I will not open it at all.

### South Window

A sunny window usually works great but it can be a challenge to get enough light. If your window is drafty, place an old towel over the sill to set the seedlings on. You can also use a heat mat; there are different sizes available.

### Grow Light

A grow light will also work fine, though your seedlings may not be as healthy as sun-grown plants. It will get you through until you can set the young plants outside. See page 14 for more instructions on grow lights.

### Water

Only water your seedlings when soil has become dry, but do not let plants wilt. Let soil dry out a little between

Penelope Jane
tasting seedlings as we plant

*T*hese seedlings did not get enough light as soon as they started coming up. They stretched looking for light.

watering to help prevent disease.

## Fertilizer

Water them once a week with liquid fish solution or compost tea. Seedlings LOVE compost tea!

## Disease

Damping-off disease is a common disease that attacks young seedlings in which plants rot at the soil level and fall over. Keeping the area well ventilated and letting soil dry out a little between watering will help control the disease. Using compost tea will also help keep plants healthy and prevent disease.

## Problems

What's wrong with my seedlings? They are tall and skinny and falling over!

1. Very likely your seedlings did not have enough direct sunlight. Are they leaning towards one direction? That means they are stretching to get more light. It is amazing how plants know where the light is!

2. High temperatures can also cause plants to shoot up rapidly, but more so if the lighting isn't adequate.

3. Maybe seeds were sprinkled too thick and seedlings are crowded. That will also cause them to get tall and spindly. They need a little elbow room!

If conditions are extreme, then it is hard to correct, but here are some things you can do:

1. First, give them better lighting; if you don't have a place with sun then use a grow light.

2. Keep the temperature down. I would set them outside whenever the weather permits. If it is a little cold with some wind, it will help make them stockier and strong. It is like a good workout for them! Just don't forget to bring them back inside when needed.

3. The other thing you can do is when you transplant them, plant them deeper, up to their necks. Just be careful not to break the thin stems.

If the conditions are too extreme, then start over. A lesson learned is one you do not have to learn again!

*Tip*

If you are growing them in a window, and seedlings start leaning towards the light, you can rotate them a half round every day. That will help them to grow straight.

Jeremiah James and Penelope Jane, our little entrepreneurs.

Seedling Sale

# Stage 3: *Transplanting Seedlings & Growing Plants*

Seedlings are ready to transplant as soon as they start to grow their second leaf.

Transplanting seedlings is quite fun! You see the seed germinate. It grows into a sprout that becomes a seedling. You take care of it and watch it get strong and healthy. It is amazing to see life come from a tiny, hard, brown seed growing out of the soil and into the world. I cannot help but be amazed at the intricate details of God's creation! Okay, I am getting carried away with the artistic side of Creation. Let's get back to transplanting our seedling.

See pages 22-23 on how to choose containers for your plants.

Mix Plant-tone granular fertilizer into your potting soil if desired. Fill containers with potting soil, but do not pack.

*1.* Pull up a whole clump of seedlings and disturb roots.

*2.* Pull seedlings apart.

*3.* Poke hole in the middle of a pot and plant seedling, being careful not to break the stem.

*4.* Water with full-strength fish solution or compost tea until soil is thoroughly moistened.

Transplanting is a little bit of a shock to them, so baby them a bit with optimum temperatures and sunlight, and make sure they don't dry out. Be careful not to over-water though. After a week or so, they will be established again and growing happily.

## Fertilizer

Transplants can be watered once a week with liquid fish solution or compost tea. If plants need the boost, both fertilizers can be applied each week, using one in the beginning and the other in the middle of the week.

## Water

As plants get bigger they will need more water. Make sure you let them dry out a little between watering, but try not to let the plants wilt, as it will prevent them from thriving.

## Pests

Aphids and whiteflies are common pests that attack seedlings. Your first defense is to keep seedlings well fed and growing healthily, but I know, sometimes these pests persist. See page 184 for an organic spray that will get rid of these little boogers.

## A Few More Tips

As your plants get bigger, start putting them outside again to harden-off (get used to the elements). This will get them ready to live in the garden. Make sure they get 1–2 weeks of hardening-off before being planted in the garden. Even heat-loving plants will need this; just be careful about cold temperatures.

If your plants are outgrowing their pots before you can get them planted, you may need to plant them in bigger pots. You don't want them to get root-bound. Root-bound means the roots have run out of room and are forming a thick mass along the walls of the container. Plants' growth will be stunted and they are harder to get established in the garden if they are root-bound.

Now you have successfully grown your own plants from seed, and you are ready to REALLY get your hands dirty!

*Look at those sweet potato vin grow! We had delicious potatoes big as footbal*

*Shoshanna and Shalom,*
*ages 3 and 5*

# Brownies for Dad

My older sister Shalom and I always loved playing house. Our family lived on a beautiful farm of 100 acres. We had lots of room to use our imaginations and be whatever we dreamed up.

I remember this particular day quite well. We were 5 and 7, playing in the loft of my dad's shop. It was not a modern-day shop of clean, sealed walls, doors, and windows. It was made of rough-cut wood and old, used fixtures, and was open and breezy. The windows were framed holes with plastic over them. I can still smell the wood smoke that came from the stove my grandfather picked up at an auction years before. Dad is a great woodworker and was always building cabinets or chairs, or carving spoons and bowls.

That day he was hard at work as Shalom and I watched him through the cracks of the loft walls. We were giggling with great delight. We had found a whole bucket of seed corn that the squirrels and mice had been eating. It was a cold day, perfect for brownies, we thought. With mischief in our eyes, we went to work.

> *"With thrills of mischief, we took our goods back to the shop loft that we had converted into our playhouse. Adding a little of this and a little of that, we came up with the perfect texture."*

We went up to the house and asked Mom for anything that was going bad. Our house was built better than the shop, but we always bought sale stuff, and that meant bugs were bound to be found in something out of date. With thrills of mischief, we took our goods back to the shop loft that we had converted into our playhouse. Adding a little of this and a little of that, we came up with the perfect texture. We poured it into a thin, tin baking pan. Dad had gotten a few hundred baking pans from an auction real cheap, with something else he needed. We carefully brought our pan of brownies to the house and put it in the wood-stove oven. We waited impatiently while they cooked. Finally they were done! Mom helped Shalom get them out, and we called Dad in. We were so excited we could not wipe the silly grins from our faces. "Dad, we made something special for you. BROWNIES!!!!" I said. Shalom was the sweet one of the two of us, so I made her promise not to give our secret away. She would have told him in an instant. I wanted to drag it out as long as I could. We served

him a brownie and stood there, eyes wide, watching him. He smiled and started to brag on what sweethearts we were. I was laughing inside so hard I could hardly stand it. In slow motion, his fork went into the brownie. He scooped it up, and it started for his mouth. The seconds seemed like they went on forever. When the fork was just inches from his mouth, we both screamed, "STOP! Don't eat it! It is gross! The mice were in it!" We just about died laughing, knowing we could have gotten him to eat it if we had wanted him to. We all laughed and laughed! That was one of those perfect days when you just can't wipe the stupid grin off your face. LIFE IS GOOD!

*Shoshanna at age three*

# Vegetable Groups

*These vegetable groups are for seed starting only. Some of it will not apply after the plants are planted in garden.*

*Method A*
___
lettuces

greens

*Method A*
___
tomatoes

peppers

eggplant

basil

sage

___
sweet potatoes

*Method A*
___
cabbage

broccoli

cauliflower

kohlrabi

brussels sprouts

kale

collards

Chinese cabbage, bok choy

(cole crops)

*Method A*
___
onions

leeks

chives

*Method A*
___
parsley

celery

*Method B*
___
melons

squash

cucumbers

(cucurbits)

*Method B*
___
asparagus

rhubarb

# Starting Specific Vegetables

Now let's talk about specific vegetables. I've grouped veggies that have similar growing habits for seed starting, recommended the best method for starting, and explained what is different about each group.

## Lettuces and Greens (Method A)

These plants love to be started in cooler temperatures. They will do best germinated at 55–65°. Grow seedlings a little cooler too, around 50–60°, to keep them from growing tall and stringy. Seedlings should be ready to transplant in about 2 weeks. Time from transplanting to planting in the garden is about 2–4 weeks.

## Cabbage, Cauliflower, Broccoli, Brussels Sprouts, Kohlrabi, Bok Choy, Chinese Cabbage, Kale, & Collards. (Method A)

These plants will do well germinated at 65–70°, a little cooler than average. Grow seedlings a little cooler too—around 60–65°. They will grow too quickly and get spindly if temperatures are too high. Time from seed to transplant, about 10–14 days. Time from transplant to garden, about 3–5 weeks.

## Tomatoes, Peppers, Eggplant, Basil, Sage (Method A)

Germinate and grow at average temperatures. Peppers are the most difficult to germinate, and they like the highest temperature. Don't give up on them if it takes them a little longer to pop up. Takes about 2 weeks from seed to transplant (peppers a little longer). Tomatoes will take 4–6 weeks from transplant to garden, while peppers, eggplant, basil, and sage are relatively slow growers and will take 7–8 weeks.

## Onions, Leeks, Chives (Method A)

Germinate at average temperatures, but grow seedlings cooler at 55–65°. When seedlings are tall enough that they start to droop, give them a haircut. This will make them grow thicker. They will grow back, so you will want to cut them several times. You will need to start these early; the more time they have to get big and hardy, the better. Give them about 6 weeks from seed to transplant, and another 4 weeks from transplant to garden. You can keep cutting them back after you transplant them until you plant in the garden.

Note: For chives, do not transplant single plants, but plant in clumps of 6 or 8 plants per pot.

## Parsley, Celery (Method A)

These seeds are a little more difficult to start and need consistent average (or a little warmer) temperatures. Do not let soil dry out! Soak seeds before planting (see tip on page 41). Grow at average temperatures. Time from seed to transplant is about 3–5 weeks. From transplant to garden is about 5–6 weeks.

## Melons, Squash, Cucumbers (Method B)

Germinate at average temperatures, but keep a sharp eye out for the first shoots to come up. For squash it sometimes only takes a few days. Squash and cucumber seedlings like it a little cooler than average, while watermelons love it warm. Time from seed to garden for squash and cucumbers is about 3 weeks; melons about 4–5 weeks.

## Asparagus, Rhubarb (Method B)

Germinate at average temperatures. Soak asparagus seeds 24 hours beforehand and rhubarb 2–3 hours (see tip on page 41). Asparagus can take a long time to germinate, sometimes up to 3 weeks. Use larger, tall containers for asparagus (at least 4 inches in diameter and 6–8 inches deep) since it will grow a long root. Give asparagus about 3 months from seed to garden. If it is growing out of its pot and getting root-bound, plant it in a bigger pot.

Rhubarb seeds should germinate quickly. A four-inch pot is a good size to plant rhubarb in. From seed to garden it will take about 4–6 weeks. Grow these seedlings at average temperatures or a little cooler.

## Sweet Potatoes

Sweet potatoes are not started from seed but by planting a sweet potato in a pot of soil. The potato will sprout and grow little shoots that will become your new plants. To start out, you can buy plants (slips) or you can buy an heirloom sweet potato or two from a farmers' market or a neighbor who grows sweet potatoes. Do not use potatoes from the supermarket—they will likely be from hybrid plants and won't produce. Plant the potato in a pot that is at least an inch bigger all around than the sweet potato, using good garden soil. Water well. You do not need drainage holes because the potato likes it wet. Put in a sunny window, though it doesn't need full sun. Will do well at room temperature. When the slips or plants are about 2–3 inches tall, carefully twist them off at the roots, and stick them in a glass with 1–2 inches of water. This will cause them to grow roots. You can then transplant them into little pots with potting soil like normal seedlings to get them established before planting in the garden.

# Homegrown Kids

*" . . . at that moment I was making something more important. I was making homegrown kids."*

The other day I was out planting seeds. Jeremiah James (my 7-year-old son) and Penelope Jane (my 2-year-old daughter) came out to help me plant. Sometimes it can be more work with them helping than with them playing. Well, most of the time it is more work! Before I knew it, the soil was flying and seeds were scat-tered. I was not sure if I planted cel-ery or lettuce. Then I smiled. I might need to plant everything again, but at that moment I was making some-thing more important—I was making homegrown kids. That is what my mom and dad did with me. I have the best memories of working and learning side by side with my parents. What I learned as a child inspired my soul and lit a fire in me that burns, a desire to go beyond what I am and what I know, and to be what I am inspired to be. The celery did come up and it is looking awesome!

# Spring Vegetables

*S*ome of my best memories are of working the garden with my dad in the spring. I can still feel the cool soil between my toes as we dug our early potatoes, and I can still taste that fresh flavor you only get when you cook vegetables the day you dig them. There is nothing like spring vegetables!

*Note:* I will be using the term 'good garden soil' throughout the Spring Vegetable section. See pages 163-170 for definition of good garden soil.

# Asparagus

*I* love the tender stems of asparagus! Nothing says spring quite like them. I remember the first time I ever had asparagus. I was helping out a local mother with her children one day. We worked in their garden and picked fresh asparagus. For supper we steamed it and topped it with a little cheddar cheese. Oh, I have been hooked ever since! Yum!

**Starting**  Asparagus can be started from seed, or you can buy one-year-old crowns (roots) from a nursery. It is super easy to start asparagus from seed! It will just take a little longer until you can harvest them. Starting seeds early in midwinter will give you a better chance at being able to harvest in the second year, and who doesn't want to eat this tasty vegetable as soon as possible? Check out Seed Starting in the previous chapter to learn how to start seeds indoors. (Specific details are on page 57.)

**Soil**  Needs good garden soil that drains well.

**Sun**  Likes full sun, but will tolerate some shade.

**Temperature**  Cool, early spring through early summer. Asparagus is one of the first veggies to pop up in the spring!

**Space & Rows**  Plant asparagus 12–18 inches apart in rows 3 feet apart if you want more than one row.

**Planting & Growing**  In northern regions, plant asparagus in spring after severe frost is past. For southern regions, it is good to plant it in the fall if you are planting crowns. This will give roots time to establish so they can tolerate the hot summer weather.

## Planting Crowns

1. Dig a trench 12 inches wide and 12 inches deep.

2. Make a little volcano mound of soil that is about 8 inches high. Then drape root over top. Continue until your row is done.

3. Fill trench with soil until crown is covered by about 2 inches.

4. As the spears start to grow, continue to fill soil around them until trench is level with the soil. Check out page 60 for information on planting asparagus seedlings.

*Water* Make sure your new asparagus bed gets well watered until it is established. After the first year or two, the roots will grow down deep and the plants will be able to take care of themselves.

*Fertilizing* Asparagus is a heavy feeder. It will need all three standard fertilizer ingredients (NPK), especially extra nitrogen. Learn more about NPK on pages 177-178.

**Asparagus** seedlings do not have many roots, so they do not need to be planted quite as deep as the crowns. Dig a hole 6–8 inches deep. Drop in the seedling and fill soil around it. After seedlings grow a little more, add a layer of compost.

**Pests & Disease** Asparagus is rarely bothered by pests and disease, but sometimes asparagus beetles can be a problem. Check out pages 183-184 for information on controlling pests and disease.

**Weeding** It is very important to keep down the weeds in your asparagus bed. Keep it well mulched and pull any stray weeds that come up.

**Harvesting** If you start your own seeds, it will take until the second or third year before your asparagus is ready to harvest. If you plant 1-year-old crowns, you should be able to pick the first spears in the second year. Harvest spears when they are 5–8 inches long. You can either cut them with a sharp knife right above the soil level, or you can just break them off; they will snap easily. You should be able to harvest spears over a period of 5–8 weeks once your bed is established. These little spears grow fast, so you will have to harvest them almost every day. After a while the new spears will start to be thinner in diameter. Let these grow into plants, since they are needed to make energy for the roots.

**Storage** Asparagus tastes best right after it is harvested. If you need to keep it for a while, place it upright in a pan with about an inch of water, and put it in the fridge. It should keep for about a week. Check out *Making Vegetables Volume 2* for information on how to freeze asparagus.

**Good Varieties**
- Mary Washington – Popular old-fashioned variety.
- Purple Passion – Sweet and tender. (There is also a hybrid version of this one; make sure you get the heirloom one!)
- Conover's Colossal – Fat and prolific.

**Notes** Asparagus plants are male and female. The female plant produces bright red berries later in the summer, and therefore does not have as much energy to put into growing spears. You may want to remove most of the female plants and replace them with male plants, which are more productive. Hybrid varieties that are available are all male plants, so they will not produce any seed.

# Cabbage & Its Family

Cabbage, Cauliflower, Broccoli, Brussels Sprouts,
Kale, Collards, Kohlrabi, Bok Choy, Chinese Cabbage

**Starting**  Start from seed indoors. Check out Seed Starting in the previous chapter to learn how to start seeds indoors. (Specific details are on page 55.)

**Soil**  Needs good garden soil with lots of organic matter.

**Sun**  They love it! Full sun will help them grow, but they tolerate light shade.

**Temperature**  Loves the cool weather, around 60–65°. Grow in spring and early summer, and again in fall through early winter.

## Space & Rows

Plants should be at least 10–12 inches apart for cabbage. Most people grow cabbage 12–18 inches apart, but planting them closer together can increase and even double your harvest. Plant brussels sprouts 16–18 inches apart, and the rest of the cabbage family 12–16 inches apart. Broccoli, cauliflower, and kohlrabi should be planted 12–16 inches apart, and brussels sprouts 16–18 inches apart. You can plant a double or triple row, offsetting the plants, to make a wide row and save space. Space between rows for walking should be 2–3 feet.

## Water

Water well in the beginning stages of growth, then slack off.

## Fertilizing

It is good to add manure to your soil in the fall, then add some lime in the spring a month or two before planting. Plants in the cabbage family do not like acidic soil, and the lime will help raise the pH. As a general guide, use 5 pounds of lime for every 100 square feet of garden area.

Plants in the cabbage family are heavy feeders, so you will need to provide plenty of nutrients to ensure success. Mix up some garden fertilizer (see pages 177-178) with extra nitrogen to apply just before planting. These plants also love compost tea.

## Planting & Growing

These plants will need firm soil to be able to support their own weight. Tamp down the soil firmly before planting to remove all air pockets. Seedlings can be planted in the garden 3–4 weeks before the last frost. You will have a lot less trouble with pests if you grow them in cool weather.

Grow these crops in the fall for winter storage in the root cellar. Cold weather and even a light frost will not hurt these plants; in fact, it will add to their flavor. Throw a blanket or plastic over them if you expect a heavier freeze. If you live in warmer climates, you might want to grow them during winter months.

>>

## Pests & Disease

Pests and diseases love cabbage and their family members, but thankfully they are cold crops. Bugs hate the cold, so as long as you grow them in the colder months, you should not have many problems. Cabbage loopers are probably the most common pests that attack these plants. Check out pages 183-184 on organic pest and disease control. Sometimes the leaves on the bottom of the brussels sprout plants turn yellow. If they do, you want to pluck them off. They can carry fungus that will spread to other plants.

## Weeding

Mulch to prevent weeds from growing. Mix some grass clippings or other green stuff into your mulch to give the plants an extra boost of nitrogen.

## Harvesting

Chinese cabbage is ready to harvest when it is the size of a football. Cabbage heads are ready to harvest anytime after they form and become firm. A light frost even sweetens the flavor, so don't rush the harvest. Cut them below the fruit, leaving a small knob of stem, or just pull the whole plant up.

Brussels sprouts can be harvested from the bottom up as they grow. They are ready to eat when firm. Brussels sprouts taste best after a few freezes. If the temperature drops below 25°, then you need to pull the whole plant up for storage.

Cut off main broccoli heads before they flower. Side shoots will continue to give a harvest for up to two months. You can also trim off the tender side greens for dinner.

Cut cauliflower when it has a firm head but has not separated. After the head separates, the clusters will start to turn yellow or brown. That means they are overripe.

Kohlrabi are ready to harvest when they are 2–4 inches in diameter. If they get too big, they will become woody and tough, or they might split.

Kale and collards can be picked as leaves grow.

## Storage

In the spring, these crops are good to eat as they ripen. Check out *Making Vegetables Volume 3* on how to store your fall crops for the winter.

>>

Do not plant any of the cabbage family in the same spot two years in a row. Plant them where the tomatoes or peppers were the year before. This helps to protect them from pests and disease.

*Good Varieties*

Cabbage:
- Mammoth Red Rock – Hardy, large red cabbage that does well in storage.
- Golden Acre – Small, early green cabbage; great for small gardens.
- Premium Late Flat Dutch – Giant green cabbage; great for storage.

Chinese Cabbage:
- Michihili – Dark green variety with crisp interior.

Bok Choy:
- Canton Bok – Baby type: more heat tolerant.

Broccoli:
- Calabrese Green Sprouting – Will produce medium-size heads with many side shoots.
- De Cicco – Very early; also great for freezing.

Cauliflower:
- Snowball Self-Blanching – An old favorite that will grow leaves to blanch itself.
- Purple of Sicily – Great tasting, beautiful purple heads that are rich in minerals; cooks to a bright green.

Brussels Sprouts:
- Long Island Improved – Good old-fashioned variety.

Kohlrabi:
- Purple Vienna and White Vienna – Good early varieties.
- Giant White or Superschmelz – Grows delicious, gigantic bulbs.

Kale:
- Blue Curled Scotch – Compact plants grow tender blue-green leaves that are crinkled and delicious.

Collards

- Morris Heading – Popular heirloom, fast grower.

*Notes*  If you live in a milder climate, you can succession plant these to have a crop all winter long.

Red cabbage stores a little better than green, but don't just plant the reds, because some of the green ones are really tasty.

When cauliflower heads start emerging out of the leaves and getting exposed to the sun, they need to be protected. Sunburn will cause them to become bitter. Pull the leaves together over the heads and tie with a string or slip on a rubber band. This will block the sun and blanch them to a creamy white. Check on them every couple days, since heads can grow fast, depending on the weather. In warmer weather it could take 4–6 days; in cooler weather, up to 2 weeks.

Brussels sprouts need a fairly long growing season and are best planted in early to midsummer for a late fall/early winter harvest.

Broccoli beginning to flower (*top left*)
Cabbage (*top right*)
Purple kohlrabi (*bottom right*)

# Celery & Parsley

I have about 30 plants of celery in my greenhouse right now. We juice them every morning. Fresh and delicious! A little fresh parsley dresses up any dish. It is a great herb to have all year long!

**Starting** Start from seed indoors. Check out Seed Starting in the previous chapter to learn how to start seeds indoors. (Specific details are on page 57.)

**Soil** Likes good garden soil, high in nutrients.

**Sun** Best planted where it will get afternoon shade, especially in hot areas.

**Temperature** These plants love the cool weather, but parsley is the more adaptable of the two, growing well in both hot and cold temperatures. Celery is pretty picky about temperature; it does not stand frost like parsley, and doesn't hold up as well in the heat.

**Space & Rows** Plant celery 8–12 inches apart in rows 18–24 inches apart. Double rows work great for celery. Plant parsley 18–24 inches apart, since it can get big! You will get a lot from one plant. Parsley is also great to grow in a container.

| *Water* | They both like consistent water, but celery is especially picky! It needs consistent water to grow crisp and tasty. |
|---|---|
| *Fertilizing* | Celery is a heavy feeder, so make sure to supply nutrients as needed. Add all-purpose garden fertilizer before planting and during the growing season. Parsley likes good food too, but is not as finicky. |
| *Planting & Growing* | For a spring crop, plant right after danger of frost is past (parsley can be planted earlier). If celery grows well, you should be able to harvest some before the weather gets hot. If celery (or parsley) seems to die back during the hot summer months, do not pull it up; it will very likely re-grow in the fall. In hot climates, you might want to skip spring planting and plant celery in July for a fall crop. |
| *Pests & Disease* | Celery can be attacked by numerous pests. Once again, healthy soil and regular applications of compost tea are your first defense. Check out pages 183-184 for organic bug spray if needed. |
| *Weeding* | Mulch these plants with wood chip mulch to avoid weeds. Mix in some grass clippings or other green material to give a little more nitrogen. |
| *Harvesting* | Celery is ready to harvest any time after it has grown stalks, either by cutting single stalks as you need them, or by cutting the whole plant about an inch above soil level. If weather is still warm, the root stub will grow out again, so don't pull it up. Note: Unblanched celery is greener and higher in nutrition then blanched celery. If you prefer to blanch it, tie newspapers or paper bags around the stalks before harvesting. Blanching may take 10–14 days. Celery does not stand frost, so be sure to harvest before the first frost.<br><br>Harvest parsley by picking the leaves as needed throughout the growing season. |

>>

Celery in the green-house with drip line at the famous French Laundry

**Storage**

Celery and parsley will keep in the fridge for 7–10 days. Celery can also be stored in the root cellar. Check out *Making Vegetables Volume 3* for information on how to store.

**Crop Rotation**

Be sure to rotate any member of the carrot family (carrots, celery, cilantro, parsley, dill, etc.) every year to avoid pest and disease problems.

**Good Varieties**

Parsley:

- Giant of Italy – Good Italian flat leaf.
- Triple Curled – Great for garnishing.

Celery:

- Golden Self-Blanching – Popular variety, easy to blanch.
- Tendercrisp – Large celery with excellent flavor.

**Notes**

Parsley is very cold-hardy and can be overwintered in many areas. Mulch over well in colder regions.

# Cilantro

| | |
|---|---|
| *Starting* | Start from seed. See Planting and Growing information on the following page. |
| *Soil* | Plant cilantro in good, well-drained garden soil. |
| *Sun* | Full sun to partial shade. |
| *Temperature* | Cool weather crop; tends to bolt in the hot summer. |
| *Space & Rows* | Give cilantro plants about 6 inches of space in every direction. |
| *Water* | Likes even moisture. |
| *Fertilizing* | Does not need much extra fertilizer. |

## Planting & Growing

Cilantro does not like to be transplanted, so it is best to plant seeds directly in the garden or in pots. Plant seeds in spring, after danger of frost has passed. Prepare a bed of fine soil, lay seeds on top of soil, and poke down ½ inch with your finger. Water gently.

## Pests & Disease

Cilantro is pretty hardy, so you shouldn't have any problems. The best treatment is prevention, and the best prevention is to start with healthy soil.

## Weeding

Keep free of weeds. A light, wood chip mulch will help keep weeds down.

## Harvesting

You can start picking the outer leaves as soon as there is a nice bunch of them. If the plant starts to bolt, cut off the whole center stem that is bolting. Harvesting regularly will encourage fresh, new leaves to keep growing.

## Storage

Cilantro is best used right after it is picked, but will keep in the fridge for 3–4 days. Rinse with water to moisten it before storing in the fridge, and it will stay fresh longer.

## Crop Rotation

If you have problems with pests or disease, do not plant cilantro or any other member of the carrot family in the same spot two years in a row.

## Good Varieties

- Slow Bolt – As its name implies, this variety is slower to bolt so it is more suitable for warmer climates.
- Leisure – Grown for its large, glossy green leaves.

## Notes

Your spring crop of cilantro will bolt and go to seed as soon as the weather gets hot. The seeds it produces are coriander seeds and can be used in cooking, or you can just let them go, and they will reseed for a fall crop. To save seeds, cut off seed heads when seeds have turned brown but before they fall to the ground. Place in a paper bag and let dry in a nice airy spot. After several weeks, pick off remaining seeds and store in an airtight container.

# Greens

## Lettuce, Spinach, Arugula, Mustard Greens, and Other Greens

*T*here are tons of different greens that make great salads. We have many different kinds of lettuces from leafy (also called "cut and come again" because of their ability to continue producing after being cut) to head varieties such as romaine, butterhead, and iceberg. Then there are all the other greens such as spinach, cress, arugula, and mustards.

*Starting*  Start from seed; it's super easy! You can sow directly in the garden, or get an early start by starting head lettuce indoors. Check out Seed Starting in the previous chapter to learn how to start seeds indoors. (Specific details are on page 55.)

*Soil*  Lettuces and greens prefer soil high in organic matter with good water-holding capacities.

*Sun*  These plants will do okay in full sun in spring and fall, but they prefer some shade in the afternoon during the warmer months.

**Temperature** They like it cool, between 50° and 65°. They can be grown in cooler temps too, and will survive temperatures as cold as 28°. Hot temperatures will cause them to taste bitter, bolt, and go to seed. In warmer climates you can grow them in the winter, and in cooler climates, grow them spring through fall.

**Space & Rows** For head lettuces, transplant seedlings 8–12 inches apart, depending on how big the variety will get. Romaine and butterheads need about 8 inches, and iceberg heads need 12 inches. Plant double or triple rows to save space.

**Water** When seeds are freshly sown in the garden, mist them well once a day or as often as the soil dries out. Keep an eye on them, and don't let them get bone dry. After seeds are up, keep soil consistently moist. If they dry out, it can stunt their growth and cause them to become bitter.

**Fertilizing** Add compost to your soil before planting them. Greens like lots of nitrogen. If they don't get enough, they will not grow fast and rich in greenness. They are GREENS remember? Nitrogen = GREEN! However, too much nitrogen can make them bitter, so don't overdo it. Manure is a great way to green up your greens. Work about an inch of composted manure into your soil before planting. To give plants a boost, check out high-nitrogen fertilizers on pages 177-178.

>>

Jeremiah James
my gardening buddy

## Planting & Growing

Head lettuce seedlings can be planted 2–3 weeks before the last frost. Direct sowing in the garden or hotbed can be done up to 4 weeks before the last frost (in a hotbed even earlier). Sprinkle seeds loosely over fine, even soil. Cover with fine compost or good garden soil. Water gently. Seeds should come up in 3–7 days, depending on the temperature.

For leaf lettuce, spinach, and other greens, seedlings can be fairly crowded, but if too crowded they will be tall and spindly. If needed, you can thin the seedlings by hand; or using a rake, gently rake through the seedlings. This is a fast way to thin a large area of them. If you planted a head variety, seedlings can be transplanted when they have two true leaves.

Lettuce is great to "succession plant." Plant every 10–14 days for a full and continuing crop.

## Pests & Disease

Lettuce and other greens do not seem to have a lot of pest and disease problems; however, animals like to eat them. If you are having trouble with this, you can put up a fence, make a row cover with arched wire and garden fleece (see page 199), or you can try planting marigolds around your greens; rabbits especially do not like marigolds.

## Weeding

You can mulch head lettuces to prevent weeds. Leafy lettuces and greens can be more of a challenge. Start out with weed-free soil, and it will help immensely. If weeds do come up, hand weed right away, being careful not to disturb plants too much.

## Harvesting

Leafy lettuces are ready to harvest when they are about 3 to 4 inches tall. The small leaves are more tender and sweet. Cut one inch above the ground and within a week or two it will have re-sprouted. If kept well picked, you can get quite a few harvests off the same bed. Head lettuce is ready to harvest when heads are firm. Do not wait too long; heads might bolt. Some butterheads do not form much of a head, but will be more like a large cluster of leaves.

>>

*Storage* Lettuce is one thing that does not store well. You can store iceberg and romaine heads for a short time, wrapped in a cotton cloth in the root cellar. The nice thing is that lettuce loves cool weather, and you can have it all winter in a hotbox or greenhouse. You might even be able to grow some in the shade in summer. Spinach is easy to grow all winter long, and stores well. Blanching and freezing it keeps it fresh tasting and easy to use. See *Making Vegetables Volume 2* for freezing instructions.

*Crop Rotation* Crop rotation is not really needed for most leafy greens. However, If you have trouble with pests and disease, you can always relocate next year. Pests like to come back to the same spot where they got good food the year before.

*Good Varieties* Lettuce:

- Red Romaine – A good romaine head.
- Lolla Rosa Darkness – Lovely, red, loose-leaf with heavily fringed leaves.
- Black Seeded Simpson – Very popular green leaf variety; stands heat.
- Little Gem – Tasty little green romaine that does well in heat or cold.
- Amish Deer Tongue – Great for loose-leaf or small, compact green heads.
- Rocky Top Lettuce Mix – Mixture of loose-leaf lettuces; great for cut-and-come-again lettuce.

Spinach:

- Bloomsdale Long Standing – Old heirloom variety; does well in hot weather.

*Notes* Turnip greens, mustard greens, and kale are good cover crops. Growing up in Tennessee, our winters were not too harsh. My parents planted these greens over our entire garden every winter, and we ate them all winter long.

Hot temperatures will cause greens to bolt and go to seed, but there are still uses for them if that happens. Arugula and mustard flowers are tasty in salads.

Penelope Jane
eating her greens

# New Potatoes

If you have never had a fresh new potato cooked straight from the ground, you just don't know what you are missing. Soft, creamy, rich, and succulent, they melt in your mouth. New potatoes are dug when the potato is still small. I love them best washed and steamed, with sea salt, pepper, and butter. YUM!

**Starting** Potato plants are started by planting tubers (small potatoes). Be sure to buy certified, disease-free seed potatoes from a good supplier, since potatoes from the supermarket may carry viruses. Seed potatoes can be cut into multiple pieces as long as there are several little buds or "eyes" on each piece.

**Soil** Potatoes like good garden soil that drains well. They do not like soggy soil.

**Sun** Full sun for best yield; tolerates partial shade.

**Temperature**

Potato plants stand a little frost, so you can start your first crop early. They also do well throughout the summer.

**Space & Rows**

Plant 8 inches apart in rows 2–2½ feet apart.

**Water**

Moderate, even moisture. They do not like too much water.

**Fertilizing**

Potatoes like fertilizer with a little less nitrogen – more phosphorus and potassium. Humus and compost are great for potatoes. Too much composted manure can cause scab disease, which creates rough patches on the skin. Check out page 173 to make your own root crop fertilizer. They also love to be mulched with wood chips.

**Planting & Growing**

Your first potato crop can be planted 2–3 weeks before the last frost. Using a hoe, dig a row about 4–6 inches deep. Place seed potatoes in the row, eyes facing up. Cover with soil, about 4 inches. As potato plants start to pop out of the ground, you can either apply several inches of mulch, or hill them up with soil (rake up the soil to the base of the plant) before you apply the mulch. This will give them more room to grow tubers, and it will keep the tubers from getting exposed to the sun. Exposure to the sun will turn potatoes green, which makes them toxic.

**Pests & Disease**

Colorado potato beetle and the dark orange grub are two of the main pests that love potatoes. These bugs are often hand picked off the plant. Check out pages 183-184 for pest and disease control. Most viruses and diseases can be prevented by using disease-free seed potatoes, and by rotating crops.

**Weeding**

Weeds shouldn't be a problem when mulched with wood chips.

>>

New
Potatoes

## Harvesting

New potatoes are ready to harvest after plants have flowered, approximately 60 days after planting. They are great to dig as you need them. Using a pitchfork, dig up the soil starting about a foot away from the plant, being careful not to damage your potatoes.

## Storage

New potatoes are best eaten when they are freshly dug; however, they will keep several months in a root cellar.

## Crop Rotation

Do not plant potatoes where tomatoes or potatoes were grown in the past three years.

## Good Varieties

- Dark Red Norland – One of the earliest varieties; good for warm and cold climates.

- Purple Majesty – Blue inside and out, lots of fun, and loaded with antioxidants.

- Yukon Gold – An early variety, and also a good keeper; great all-purpose potato.

# Onions & Family

There are so many different members of the onion family: garlic; leeks; green, red, and white onions; and many others. When you have so many options, it is easy to take your food from ordinary to gourmet! Yum! I love good food!

**Starting**  There are basically three different ways to start onions. You can buy onion sets or onion transplants, or start your onions from seed. Onion sets are little onion bulbs that were grown the year before. Transplants are little onion plants that were started from seed. If you start from seed, you will need to get an early start. Check out Seed Starting in the previous chapter to learn how to start seeds indoors. (Specific details are on page 56.)

**Soil**  Soil should be well drained and rich with plenty of organic matter.

**Sun**  Plant in full sun. SUN, SUN, SUN! They like 8–16 hours of sun a day.

**Temperature**  Onions are very cold-hardy, and they need to be planted early, up to four weeks before the last frost date. Green onions can be planted and grown throughout the summer.

**Space & Rows**  Plant onions 6–8 inches apart in rows 12 inches apart.

*Water* Onions don't need to be drenched in water but they need water all the time. They have shallow roots; so a little water goes a long way. Watering is especially important in the first few weeks after planting. Water every few days until plants are established. Mulching will help retain moisture as well.

*Fertilizing* Because onions have shallow roots, they need to have good soil and, if needed, a little humus or organic garden fertilizer for nutrients. The key to fertilizing is this: nitrogen will grow big green tops and small root bulbs, and phosphorus will help grow big bulbs.

*Planting & Growing* Plant onion transplants about ½ inch deep (make sure the tiny bulb is down about ½ inch). Plant onion sets with the root end down and make sure the little tips sticking out are just barely covered.

*Pests & Disease* Onions are rarely bothered by pests and diseases. In some areas onion thrips can be a problem though, so look out for small, brown worms that eat holes in the leaves to suck up the sap. Signs of attack are bent leaves with small, silvery-gray spots. Check out pages 183-184 for pest control.

*Weeding* Onions cannot compete with weeds, so be sure to keep them weed-free. Of course the fabulous wood chip mulch will do most of the work for you!

*Harvesting* Harvest onions when most of the tops have fallen over, mid-summer to early fall in most areas. Pull up plants carefully, or dig with a pitchfork. Leave them in the sun for a few days, and then transfer to a well-ventilated shed or garage for another 10–14 days of curing. Onions can be braided and hung up, or spread out in a single layer to cure.

*Storage* Onions can be stored for many months if given proper care. Check out *Making Vegetables Volume 3* for information on how to store onions for the winter.

>>

**Crop Rotation**

Rotate onion crops at least every 2 to 4 years. Plant them where root crops have not grown the year before.

**Good Varieties**

Plant long-day varieties in the north and short-day varieties in the south. Long-day varieties need 14–16 hours of daylight to grow big bulbs, while short-day varieties need no more than 12 hours.

Long-day varieties for the north:

- Yellow Sweet Spanish – Large onion; good keeper.
- Noordhollandse Bloedrode (Dutch Red) – Large, slightly flat onion; good keeper.

Short-day varieties for the south:

- Red Creole – Spicy red onion that keeps well.
- Valencia – Large, mild, yellow onions that are adaptable for short- or long-day regions. Also makes good green onions when young.

**Notes**

Your onion plant will put its energy into growing a big green top while the days are still short. As the days get longer, more sun triggers the onion to put its energy into making a bulb. The bigger the top, the bigger the bulb will be!

You can use transplants or sets to grow big onions, but since the sets are already a year old, they will not store as well.

# Green Onions or Scallions

As a girl, I practically lived outside picking wild plants. Wild green onions were everywhere. I would pick them mostly for Susanna Beachy. She taught me a lot about plants, and she loved to cook with them.

Green onions are one of the earliest veggies to plant in your garden. If you have a bunch of onions left over from last year that are starting to sprout, go ahead and stick them in your early garden and soon you will have three or four delicious green onions growing out of each old onion.

You can also grow green onions from seed (regular onion seed works fine) or onion sets. Just grow like normal onions, but plant them closer together, about 2 inches apart in rows 3 inches apart. Harvest when they get as big as you want them!

*Tip:*

Try directly sowing seeds in the garden after the soil has warmed and is workable. Thin out seedlings so that each one has room to grow as big as you want them. Sow every 3–4 weeks for a continual supply.

Try Red Welsh Bunching Onion, a perennial onion that does not bulb, but produces side shoots that can be replanted. Get this one established, and you will have a constant supply of green onions!

# Leeks

Leeks are grown just like onions, except for the way they are planted. Start by digging a trench that is 4–6 inches deep. Plant leeks in the trench and then gradually fill in the trench as they grow to get nice, white, blanched stems. Leeks do not keep well after they are harvested, so leave them in the ground until you need them. They are very cold-hardy, so you can leave them in the garden right into the winter.

*Good Varieties*

- Giant Musselburgh – large with very thick stems; tasty and mild.

>>

# Chives

*Starting*  Start chive seeds like onions (see page 56). Chives are perennial, so they will come back every year and will keep on multiplying. They will grow back when you harvest the leaves during the summer, so a few clumps will go a long way. You can also dig up part of an old clump to get starts for new plants.

*Good Varieties*
- Chives Common – Normal chives that produce purple, edible flowers, usually the second year.
- Chives Garlic – Chives with a distinct garlic flavor. Produces gorgeous white flowers that are great in salads.

# Garlic

Garlic is grown similarly to onions, but there are a few minor differences.

*Starting*  Garlic is always started by planting cloves. For your first planting, it is better to buy disease-free garlic from a good supplier than to plant garlic from the supermarket.

*Planting & Growing*  Garlic needs to go through a cold period to form big bulbs, so in most areas it needs to be planted in the fall. You can plant it in the spring, but it will not grow as big. Carefully separate the cloves and push them into the soil, pointed end up, until the tips are barely covered. Add an inch of compost on top of the garlic bed. If you don't add compost, push cloves down a little deeper. Put 2–3 inches of mulch on top to protect over the winter.

*Space & Rows*  Plant 6 inches apart in rows 8–12 inches apart.

*Harvesting* Garlic is ready to harvest when the bottom 2 or 3 leaves turn brown. Gently dig up with a pitchfork, brush off the dirt, and hang in bunches in a well-ventilated shed or garage for about 2 weeks. Check out *Making Vegetables Volume 3* for information on how to store garlic.

*Good Varieties* There are two different kinds of garlic: hardneck and softneck. Hardneck varieties are hardier, which makes them great for colder areas. They have bigger cloves, but they do not store as well. Softneck varieties have smaller cloves, and are best for long-term storage.

Hardneck varieties will grow a stalk called a scape that has a seed pod on the end. When the scape is about 12 inches long, cut it off and it will help your bulb grow bigger. Scapes are expensive in supermarkets, so be sure to use them in the kitchen!

- Georgia Fire – Strong flavored; keeps until spring if well stored; hardneck variety.

- Chesnook Red – Large cloves; full garlic flavor; great all-around garlic; hardneck variety.

- Italian Purple (artichoke type, which means it's a softneck variety) – Great all-purpose garlic; grows almost everywhere; matures early.

*Notes* Store your largest, disease-free bulbs for next year's seed crop.

# Peas

If you have never had a fresh pea, then you have never had a pea. They are sweet, crisp, and tender, all in one bite!

**Starting**  Plant pea seeds right in the garden.

**Soil**  Peas like well-drained, good garden soil.

**Sun**  Peas yield best in full sun, but tolerate partial shade.

**Temperature**  Peas love the cool weather so plant your first crop early. They can be grown into the summer, but will not do well in extremely hot weather.

| | |
|---|---|
| *Space & Rows* | Plant two rows 6 inches apart, spacing seeds 3–4 inches apart. Put up trellising between rows for peas to grow on. |
| *Water* | Moderate until blooming, then low. Peas will turn yellow and yield poorly if soil is too wet, so make sure the soil doesn't get waterlogged. |
| *Fertilizing* | Work some manure into the soil before planting, and add a dressing of compost on top. The peas will love it! |
| *Planting & Growing* | Your first crop of peas can be planted up to 4 weeks before the last frost. Be sure to plant the Early Frosty variety first! |
| | Using a hoe, dig row about an inch deep. Place seeds in row, cover with dirt, about an inch. After plants are several inches tall, they will start to grow tendrils and need trellising. If trellising is not an option, peas can be left to grow on the ground, but might be more susceptible to mold. |
| *Pests & Disease* | Several viruses attack peas, causing yellowing, mottling, and distortion of leaves. A lot of diseases are spread by aphids, which can be avoided by having healthy soil and spraying with compost tea. Check out pages 183-184 for a pest and disease spray. |
| *Weeding* | Mulch will keep down 99% of the weeds. |
| *Harvesting* | Pick shelling peas when they are nice and plump but still sweet. Snap peas are grown for their sweet, edible pods. Pick them before the peas have developed. |
| *Storage* | Peas taste best right after they are picked. You can freeze or can them, but they are just not the same as fresh. Check out *Making Vegetables Volume 2* for information on how to freeze peas. |

>>

Peas

**Crop Rotation**  If you have trouble with disease or pests, do not plant peas where any beans or peas were the year before.

**Good Varieties**
- Early Frosty – Great early variety; stands frost.
- Green Arrow – Long pods packed with delicious, deep green peas.

# Rhubarb

**Starting**   The best way to start rhubarb is from divisions (roots that have multiplied and been divided) but you can also start it from seed. Check out Seed Starting in the previous chapter to learn how to start seeds indoors. (Specific details are on page 57.)

**Soil**   Rhubarb likes good garden soil that will not hold too much water over the winter and early spring. Soil that gets too wet will cause roots to rot.

**Sun**   Rhubarb does well in full sun, but will need some afternoon shade in warmer climates.

**Temperature**   Rhubarb loves the cool weather. It grows all over the U.S. but does better in cooler climates.

**Space & Rows**   Rhubarb will multiply, so plants will need to be spaced 3 feet apart in each direction.

**Water**   Likes even moisture, but too much water will make the roots rot.

singing
in the cellar!

Learn how to can
rhubarb in
Making Vegetables
Volume 2

## Fertilizing

Rhubarb loves lots of compost and rotted manure twice a year.

## Planting & Growing

Plant in early spring, after severe frost is past. Dig a hole 2–3 times as big as your plant. Fill hole with equal parts of soil, compost, and rotted manure; mix together. Plant rhubarb in mixture, but do not plant too deep. Allow soil to slant slightly away from the base of the plant so that water can run off. Cover whole rhubarb bed with a layer of compost, then add mulch on top.

## Pests & Disease

Rhubarb does not have many pest and disease problems.

## Weeding

Keep free of weeds. Mulching in the spring and fall will take care of most of the weeds.

## Harvesting

Do not harvest any rhubarb the first year. The second year, only harvest it lightly, and after that you can pick it as much as you want.

Rhubarb stalks can get as big as celery stalks, but you can pick them however big you want them. Either cut rhubarb stalks with a sharp knife at ground level or twist free with a sharp tug.

## Storage

Rhubarb stalks will keep for 5–6 days in the refrigerator in an airtight bag. Check out *Making Vegetables Volume 2* for instructions on how to freeze rhubarb.

## Crop Rotation

Perennial plant; do not rotate.

## Good Varieties

- Crimson Red – Bright red stalks; usually only available in roots.
- Victoria – Sweet, green to red stalks; available in seeds.

## Notes

Some rhubarb varieties will grow round stalks with flower heads up the center. Cut these off at ground level so that the plant can put its energy into growing other stalks.

Warning: Rhubarb leaves are poisonous. Do not eat!

# *Roots*
## Carrots, Beets, & Radishes

There is something to be said about root vegetables like carrots, beets, and radishes. You pull on this lusciously green plant, and then out of the ground comes a crisp and juicy root. You never get tired of doing that. It strikes a sense of awe in me. I love God's creations!

*Starting*    Root vegetables need to be directly seeded in the garden or raised bed. They do not like to be started and transplanted.

*Soil*    They like soil that is light, airy, high in organic matter, and free of rocks and pebbles. If the soil has a lot of clay, it can create oddly shaped vegetables and a strong, dirty taste. The longer your root vegetables, the deeper your soil will need to be. Carrots need about 1½–2 feet of loose, deep soil.

*Sun*    Root vegetables love lots of sun, so give them at least 6–8 hours a day of full sun.

## Temperature

Root crops thrive in cool temperatures, so grow them in early spring through early summer, and then again in the fall.

## Space & Rows

Sprinkle seeds in a strip 4–6 inches wide. Space between rows should be 8–12 inches. They can also be sown in squares or larger areas.

## Water

Keep soil moist while plants are young; water once a day if necessary. When plants are 2 to 3 inches tall, slack off watering little. The key to growing crisp, juicy roots is to provide consistent moisture so they can keep growing fast. You can overdo it though, and if you keep them too wet, roots may split.

## Fertilizing

Root crops, especially carrots, do not need a lot of extra fertilizer. If you have lots of compost or other organic matter in the soil, they should be fine. Do not use compost that is high in nitrogen like manure compost. If you need to give them a boost, use a fertilizer that is high in phosphorus and potassium.

## Planting & Growing

The first crop can be sown 3–4 weeks before the last frost. Sprinkle seed loosely over fine, even soil. Cover with about ¼ inch of vegetable compost or good garden soil. Water gently. Beets and radishes will come up in 3–7 days. Don't give up on the carrots. Sometimes they take up to 3 weeks. After plants are about an inch tall, thin them out so each root has room to grow. Picture how big you want the root to get, and make sure it has room to grow that big. You can thin the seedlings by hand, or using a rake, gently rake through the seedlings. This is a fast way to thin a large area of them.

## Pests & Diseases

Growing them in cooler weather takes care of almost any problem with these plants. When the weather gets a little warmer, sometimes radish tops get eaten. If they do, you can easily make an organic spray (pages 183-184) that will keep the bugs away.

>>

Penelope Jane loves
*carrots!*

## Weeding

Mulching root crops can be difficult, so weeds can sometimes be a problem. Starting out with weed-free soil will help. If weeds do come up, hand weed right away, being careful not to disturb plants too much.

## Harvesting

Carrots are so much fun to harvest. When they are about ¾ inch in diameter or bigger, they are ready to be harvested. Pinch your fingers around the tip of the root, then pull one way, pull the other way, then pull straight up. You have a carrot! If you are harvesting a whole bed you might want to use a pitchfork to loosen the soil and speed up the process.

Beets are delicious when they are young but you can let them grow to any size you want.

Radishes need to be pulled up before they get woody and tough. Keep an eye on them and harvest as soon as they reach the desired size.

## Storage

These root crops are easy to store. Fall crops can be stored in the root cellar for winter. Check out *Making Vegetables Volume 3* on how to store. For spring crops, harvest as you need them, or store in the fridge; they will keep up to 4 weeks. Beets are delicious pickled and canned.

## Crop Rotation

To avoid the possibility of disease, do not plant carrots where members of the carrot family were planted the year before (carrots, celery, fennel, parsley, cilantro, and dill). Do not plant beets where beets, swiss chard, or spinach were grown the year before. Radishes are less picky, but at the very least, avoid planting them in the same spot year after year.

>>

Carrots:

- Cosmic Purple – Fantastic purple carrot; kids love 'em!
- Danvers – 7- to 8-inch-long carrots; great for juicing: store well.
- Tonda Di Parigi – Small and sweet, harvest at 1–2 inches; great to grow in pots or heavier soils.

Radishes:

- French Breakfast – Delicious old heirloom with red top and white bottom.
- German Giant – Great radish; can grow large without getting woody.
- China Rose – Grows about 5 inches long; best for fall/winter.
- White Icicle – More heat tolerant.

Beets:

- Detroit Dark Red – Great for canning and fresh eating; good keeper.

*Jeremiah James eating a radish*

Radishes

# Strawberries

Strawberries are a delicious part of the spring garden. As a girl I would go and help my Amish friends pick their strawberries. They had large fields of them to sell to tourists. I have great memories of strawberry wars, running and pelting those juicy bits of goodness. We would be covered with reds spots by the end of the morning.

### Starting
Strawberries are one of the things most people prefer to buy as starter plants. Planting by seed is difficult and takes a long time. You can buy strawberry plants, which look like a root with a stub of a plant on the top.

### Soil
Strawberries like rich, well-drained soil. They seem to do well in a slightly acidic soil.

### Sun
They love the sun. Pick your strawberry spot where they will get at least 6 hours of full sun a day.

### Temperature
Strawberries prefer cool temps. They produce fruit early, and keep growing through the summer.

### Space & Rows
Plant them 18–24 inches apart. Make the rows 3–4 feet apart. This gives them room to grow and spread out. Throughout the year, runners (vines) will spread out. Keep pushing them back into their rows. The runners will root, and you can use these plants as starters for the following year.

## Water

Strawberries like water but hate to sit in it. They can easily mildew and rot if they get too much. Often you see people growing them in mounds or little hills to help with the drainage. If you are planting them in a pot, make sure you have 3 inches of gravel in the bottom and good drainage holes.

## Fertilizing

Add composted horse manure to the soil before planting. After planting, water them with liquid fish once a week for several weeks. Spreading a little humus around the plants is another great way to add nutrients. Do not fertilize plants in the fall because it will encourage new growth that winter frost will harm.

## Planting & Growing

Strawberries are best planted early, up to 3 weeks before the last frost date. Start by soaking roots in water for 30 minutes or a little more. This will help to hydrate them and give them a good start. Hint: Instead of soaking in water, soak in a liquid fish solution.

Then clean them by cutting the old leaf stubs off. If the roots are longer than 4–6 inches, snip them off. I know it sounds a little crazy to cut the roots off, but it will help them.

Then dig your hole and spread the roots out a little. Cover all the roots with dirt to the crown, but not over the top. Make sure the little promise of new growth can see the sun. Water well. Keep an eye on them in the first week or so, because they might need a little more water to get established.

As they start to grow, keep removing the flower blossoms. This will help them put their energy into the roots and plant, so you will have a better crop next year.

## Pests & Disease

Having good drainage and plenty of sun will go a long way toward preventing disease. Pests love the weak plants. A healthy plant is better able to resist pests and disease. Check out pages 183-184 on pest and disease control if needed.

>>

Jeremiah James feeding
Penelope Jane
strawberries from our
patio garden

## Weeding

Make sure to hand weed. Strawberries can be mulched with wood chip mulch, but be careful not to mulch too thickly. Use mulch that is partially rotted so that strawberry runners can root into the soil. Wood chip mulch will add life to the soil and will discourage most weeds. Occasionally after a rain, a weed will come up. Make sure you pull it when it is small. This year we have used wood chip mulch in our gardens. We have lots of garden spots, and no weeds!

## Harvesting

You will be able to harvest strawberries one year from the time you plant them. When you see that they are ripening, you will need to pick them about every 2–3 days. You can pull the strawberries off, but be careful not to pull off buds or unripe strawberries. Your harvest should last about three weeks. Normally, you will get one quart of strawberries per plant for the season.

## Storage

I love frozen strawberries! They are so good in smoothies, pies, syrups, as a frozen snack, or thawed over shortcake. Canning them for everyday use is okay, but freezing preserves their flavor best. One good way to can them is to make jam or jelly.

Check out *Making Vegetables Volume 2* on how to can and freeze your strawberries.

## Crop Rotation

It is best not to plant new strawberries where tomatoes, peppers, or other strawberries have been planted the previous year if you had any trouble with bugs. Bugs will come back to the same spot looking for a good meal!

>>

*Good Varieties*

There are two different types of strawberry varieties: June-bearing and everbearing. June-bearing plants bear once a year. They are the most popular because they give a good yield and have a larger fruit. Everbearing strawberries are a hybrid species that have been bred to produce throughout the summer. They have small fruit and bear a good yield in the first year they are planted. They will flower and set fruit whenever the temperature is between 35° and 85°.

- Best June-bearing strawberry – Honeoye
- Best everbearing strawberry – Tristar

*Notes*

In the late fall, you can get your next year's plants by digging up the root and simply cutting off the runner. Store the roots in the root cellar or under the house in a cool, dark place. They will be ready to plant in the spring.

In the winter months you can throw straw over the plants to protect them from freezing. Rake off the straw after the last spring frost.

*Tip:*

Strawberries are one of the earliest things that start growing and budding in the spring, so late frosts can be a big problem. Cover strawberries with straw or woodchip mulch in late winter while strawberries are still dormant. This will keep berries dormant a little longer, and thus avoid freezing so many of the early buds. Rake mulch off the plants after danger of frost is past. Can also be covered with row cover.

# New Plants

I spent thousands of hours of my childhood in the woods and meadows. I loved finding herbs and wild plants for my mom, friends, and for my playhouses. Mullein was the soft fuzzy leaf we called "toilet paper leaf," because it made great toilet paper! It is also great for the respiratory system, and an herb that my mom always dried for the winter.

*It was cool and dark, and the summer's heat was gone. It seemed magical to me how quickly everything changed.*

Week after week I would watch new plants come up—flowers, herbs, greens, and wild plants. I did not know what they all were, and could not believe how many there were. I was always finding a new plant that I had never seen before.

I remember one time I came across a steep north-facing hillside that was unusually shaded from the south, east, and west. It never saw the full sun. It was midday summer the first time I found the secluded little spot. From the crowded C-shape of the hill to the tall trees that hugged each other, there were just spots of light that flickered through to the dark forest below.

Stepping through the bushes that lined it, I entered a world I had never seen. It was cool and dark, and the summer's heat was gone. It seemed magical to me how quickly everything changed. There were tropical looking plants, bushes, flowers, and herbs. The steep hillside was like a bluff layered in rock shelves and rich soil. There were so many new textures, colors, and shapes. I was amazed at the shiny, thick, rubbery leaves and tropical flowers that were foreign to our climate. I wondered, "How did all the seeds get here?" The surrounding hill, rocks, and trees acted as a greenhouse in the winter cold and a shelter from the sun in the summer. I still love to go back there and look at all of the amazing plants. It was one of those moments when God took my breath away.

*Jeremiah James building his sale stand*

# Projects

*J* love building things! When I was 13, I started working in construction with my brothers a few days a week. I had been building things since I was old enough to pick up a hammer. Hard work, fresh air, and the success of making something great are exhilarating!

*Jeremiah and friends*

# *Hot Boxes*

This is a great project if you cannot make a greenhouse. This wonderful little box is self-heating. From growing seedlings and starting sweet potato plants to having lettuce all winter long, this box works!

### *Pick Your Spot.*

First you need to pick your spot. Have your box get the south sun. You want it close to the house and to be easily accessible. This will make a 2x2 hot box.

### *Materials you'll need:*

(3) 8-foot 2x10s, cedar (regular pine will work but will not last as long)

(1) 10-foot 1x2, cedar

(1) 24x26 inch sheet of plexiglass (or an old window, still in the frame)

(1) box of 3-inch outdoor deck screws

(2) piano or outdoor hinges and 1½-inch screws to attach hinges

(2) five-gallon buckets of fresh horse manure

## Step One

Dig a hole 2 feet by 2 feet by 18 inches deep.

## Step Two

Cut all boards to length and fasten together with 3-inch outdoor deck screws. Place box frame in ground and backfill the outside with dirt.

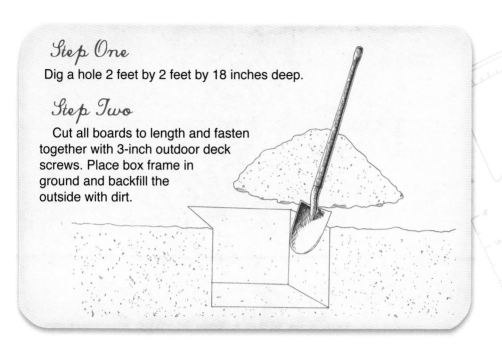

## Step Three

Build a window frame with 1x2s and attach the plexiglass window (any old window will work for this; you would just need to adjust your frame measurements accordingly)

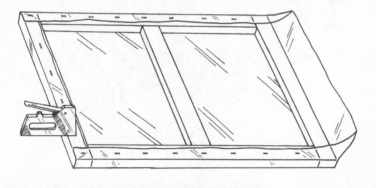

>>

## Step Four

Attach the window frame
to the box, using piano or
outdoor hinges.

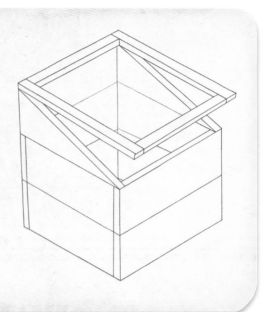

## Step Four

Put in 7 to 8 inches of fresh horse manure, then add another 8
inches of gardening soil. (This box is ideal for most winter and
spring vegetables. You can build a bigger box for larger vegetables.)

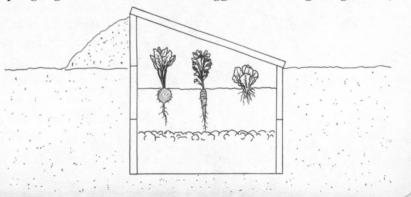

You do not have to build a fancy hot box to
have one. I have used 6 straw bales pushed
together tight with a glass door on top many
times.

# Notes

### Keep an Eye on Your Box.

If the weather forecast is calling for temperatures in the teens, I like to throw a blanket or garden fleece over the box. This just gives some extra insulation.

If the temperature rises above 50° or 60°, open the cover. The sun will quickly heat the covered box and can easily burn the plants. If it is warm in the day but calling for cold weather that night, make sure that you close the cover before it starts cooling off. It needs a little time to build up heat from the sun.

If the temperature reaches 70° or above, take the cover off completely. If you have a cold spell, don't forget to put it back on.

### Manure

There are so many kinds of manure. You need to use green manure because that is where the heat comes from. I have found horse manure works best. Read page 174 for more information on manures.

### How Long it Lasts

Hot and cold boxes are a great way to have fresh foods all winter long. This hot box will heat itself for 4–6 weeks. After that time, it will be warm for another month. The fresher the manure, the longer it will last. You can continue to use it as a cold box or clean it out and refill it with fresh manure. Cold boxes are suited for cold-loving crops like lettuces, spinach, radishes, and such.

*I* have the best greenhouse ever! My sweetheart James built it for me. I love the rough-cut cedar, the solar heat, and the fresh taste of the vegetables. The sun heats it and the ground helps it hold the warmth. I have delicious, fresh, organic vegetables in the cold winter months!

## Tools you or your contractor will need:

1. Tape measure
2. Carpenter's pencil
3. Hammer drill with bit to match concrete screws
4. Hand saw
5. Skill saw
6. Table saw with dado blade
7. Caulk gun
8. Cordless impact drill
9. Speed square
10. Framing square
11. Chalk line
12. Paintbrush
13. Drill bit set

## Materials you will need:

(24) 8-foot 2x4s, cedar

(6) 11-foot 4x4s, cedar

(4) 8-foot 4x4s, cedar

(1) box of 4-inch concrete screws

(6) 6-inch timber screws

(1) box deck screws

(50) 1½- to 2-inch roofing screws

(50) oversized galvanized rubber reinforced greenhouse washers (available from greenhouse supplier)

(1) can all-purpose PVC cement

1 to 5 gallons of flood UV coating to coat cedar boards

(6) 8-foot polycarbonate greenhouse panels (Find online or see Resources - page 278.)

(5) 11-foot polycarbonate greenhouse panels (Find online or see Resources.)

(6) 12-foot pieces of polycarbonate greenhouse H-channel

(4) 10-foot pieces of polycarbonate greenhouse U-trim

(4–5) base vents

(2–3) roof or gable vents

(10–20) tubes of Lexel® or clear silicon caulk

## Step One

Choose south-facing location and excavate the site.

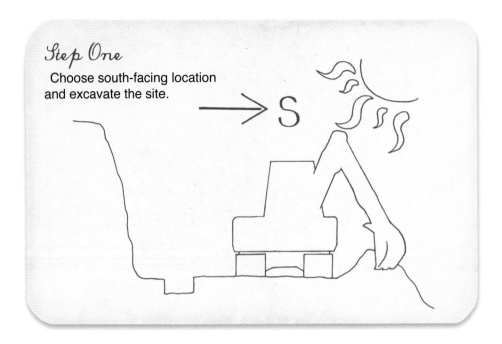

## Step Two

Dig and pour 10-inch footers where the block wall will be laid. Be sure to bend rebar to stick up past the footer 18–24 inches so it ties into the block wall.

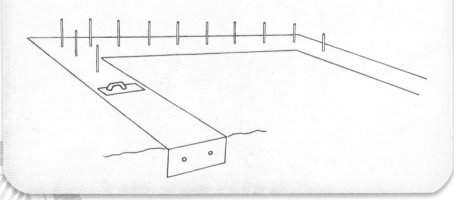

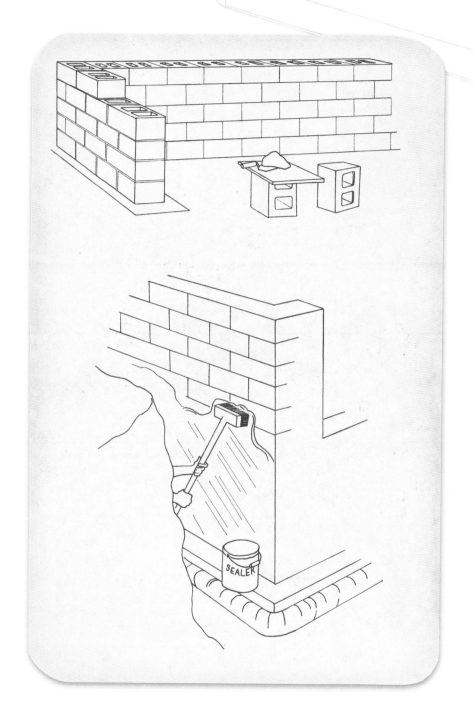

## Step Three

Lay up the block walls, laying a bond-beam layer every 3–4 feet; add rebar and pour wall solid with concrete. Waterproof the outside of the walls.

>>

## Step Four

Install perforated drainpipe at base of wall.

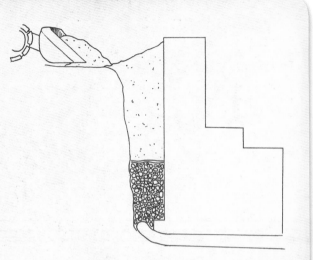

## Step Five

Backfill around the wall with 4 to 6 feet of drain gravel, cover with filter, then finish backfilling with dirt.

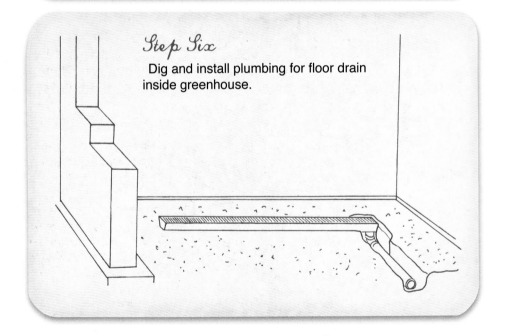

## Step Six

Dig and install plumbing for floor drain inside greenhouse.

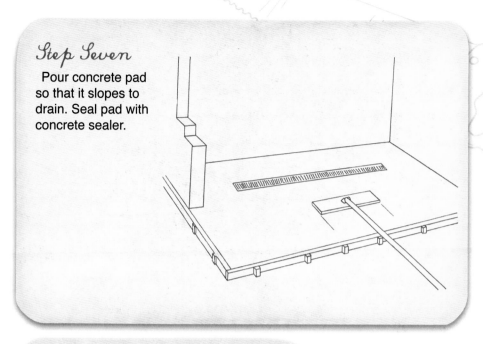

## Step Seven

Pour concrete pad so that it slopes to drain. Seal pad with concrete sealer.

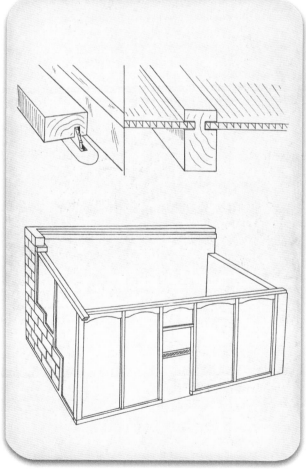

## Step Eight

Measure and cut all wall boards to length, using a dado blade to make the grooves for the polycarbonate greenhouse panels about ½ inch deep. Assemble all walls with 3-inch deck screws and fasten them in place with concrete screws. (To save time later, coat all cedar lumber with a UV sealant before assembly.)

## Step Nine

Fasten horizontal 2x6 board 2–3 inches from the top of the block wall with concrete screws.

>>

## Step Ten

Measure, cut, and install 4x4 rafters with 6-inch timber screws. Install bird blocking and cross supports between rafters. (Be sure to countersink the screws so they do not stick up above the rafters.)

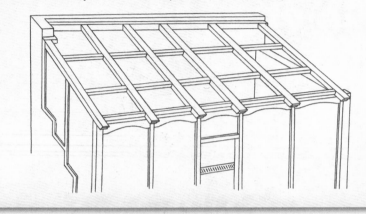

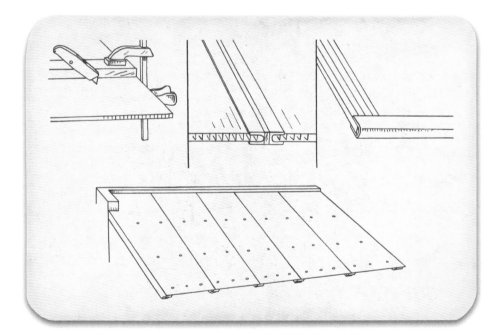

## Step Eleven

Measure, cut (with a sharp utility knife along a clamped straight edge), and install polycarbonate greenhouse roof panels using H-channel, U-trim, and 3-inch roofing screws. (Replace the roofing screw washers with larger washers from a greenhouse supply store. Also, be sure to seal off all open roof panel cavities and install polycarbonate greenhouse U-trim on the top and bottom edges—bugs love to crawl into the warm panels and lay eggs.)

## Step Twelve

Make door to fit opening or get one from the hardware store before you start the project. It is best to have one with a large window.

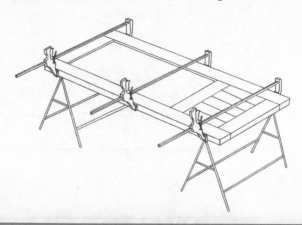

## Step Thirteen

Install base and roof vents for circulation.

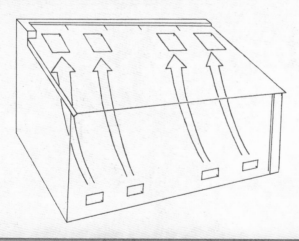

# Beds Inside Our Complex Greenhouse

*Materials you will need:*

(20) 8-foot 4x4s, cedar

(70 to 100) 6-inch timber screws

Enough 1X cedar boards to cover bottom of bed.

## Step One

Mark out wall supports for the planting bed, and attach two wall brackets to the wall with 2-inch concrete screws.

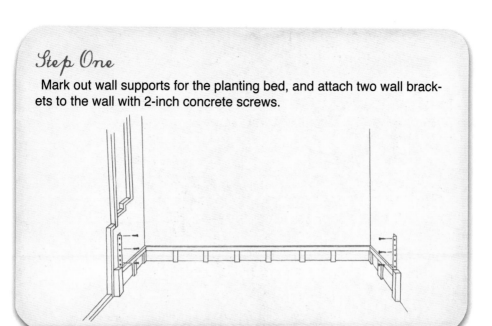

## Step Two

Cut, dado, and assemble the first row of 4x4s, leveling and bracing as you go. Fasten the corners together with 6-inch timber screws.

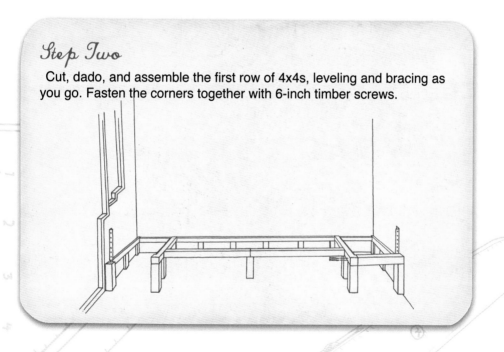

I love that this bed is tall so I do not have to bend down. It never hurts my back! Also, the space under the bed is great for storing plastic totes that hold all the greenhouse supplies!

## Step Three

Stack the next four layers of 4x4s like Lincoln Logs and fasten them together with 6-inch timber screws. (Another layer can be added to deepen the bed.)

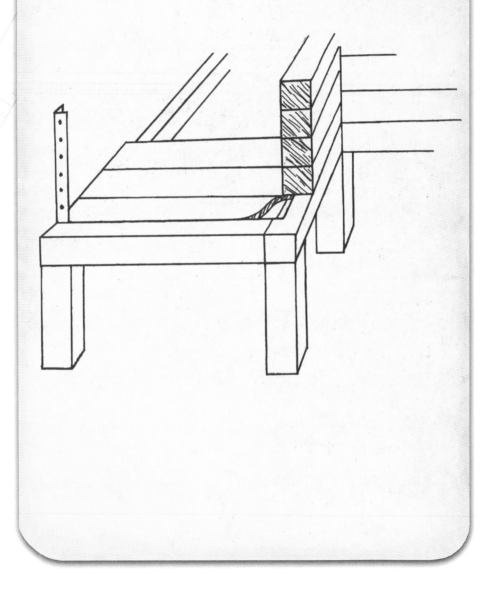

## Step Four

Cut and lay in the boards for the bottom of the bed.

## Step Five

Fill with good gardening soil.

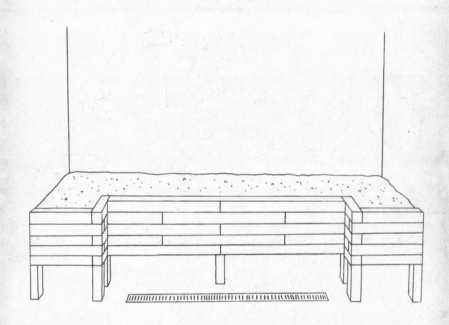

# Simple Greenhouse (Hoop House)

$\mathcal{G}$reenhouses can be intimidating. I know because I have been working on them. What to build? What to buy? How much is it going to cost? Can I do it by myself? Well, it is a lot simpler than you might think! Here are some easy, affordable, and functional greenhouses that I have enjoyed building.

## Tools you will need:

1. Tape measure
2. Hammer
3. Knife
4. Hand saw
5. Staple gun
6. Cordless drill

## Materials you will need:
(available at Lowe's or see Resources - page 276.)

(2) 10-foot ½-inch CPVC supply tubing (stakes)

(9) 10-foot ¾-inch PVC tubing (hoop frame)

(6) ¾-inch PVC couplings (hoop frame)

(1) 6-foot 1-inch black flexible PE tubing (clips)

(1) 20x24 foot sheet 4–6mil clear or translucent plastic sheeting

(4) 12-foot 2x4s

(5–10) zip ties

(14) outdoor deck screws

(1) all-purpose plumber's glue (optional)

## Step One

Choose location (south-facing, good soil, etc.) and cut all pipe to length.

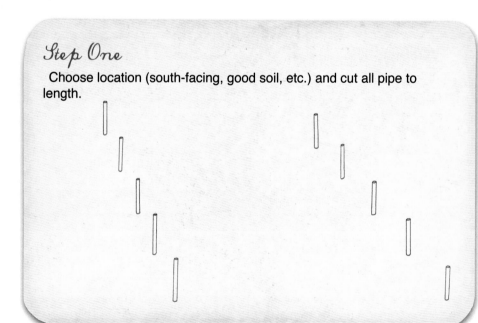

## Step Two

Measure out a 6-foot by 12-foot area and drive in ½-inch CPVC stakes every 36 inches on the 12-foot sides.

>>

## Step Three

Assemble the ¾-inch frame hoops, and zip-tie the ridge pipe to the hoops. (Joints can be glued to increase strength.)

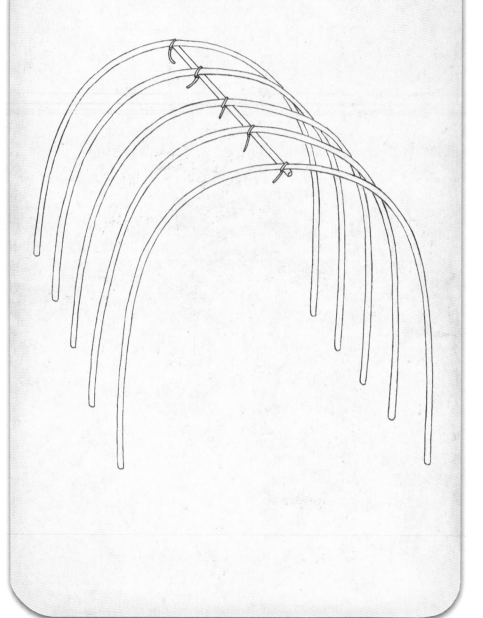

Jeremiah
picking baby arugula
for pizza

## Step Four

Cut plastic to 13x20 feet. Staple plastic to the 2x4s on one side of the hoops, sandwich it with another 2x4, and fasten the two together with 2½-inch outdoor deck screws every 2 feet or so. Stretch plastic over hoops and repeat on the other side. Attach 1-inch PE tubing clips on outside hoops to secure plastic.

## Step Five

Cut plastic for door, attach with 1in. PE tubing clips, and cut a slit in the middle for entry.

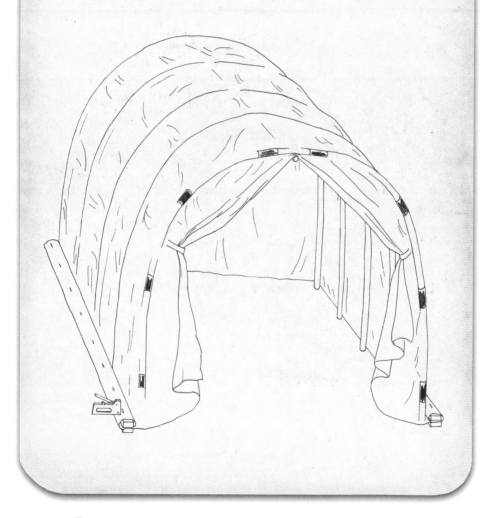

This greenhouse is great for cold-loving plants since it will not be heated.

# Greenhouse Addition

This is a nice, permanent greenhouse. I like this one because it is easy to access, and it is powered by water and electricity. Having it attached to the house helps keep it warm. Because it only has three sides, make sure your greenhouse is facing south. This will ensure that you get the best light. The sun's radiant heat will go a long way through the winter months, allowing you to heat it less.

## Tools you or your contractor will need:

1. Tape measure
2. Skill saw
3. Caulk gun
4. Cordless impact drill
5. Speed square
6. Framing square
7. Drill bit set
8. 6-foot straight edge
9. Utility knife

## Materials you will need:

(6) 12-foot 4x4s, cedar

(8) 8-foot 4x4s, cedar

(4) 12-foot 2x4s, cedar

(16) 8-foot 2x4s, cedar

(12) 6-inch timber screws

(1) box 3-inch deck screws

(1) storm door or materials for the equivalent

(6) 8-foot polycarbonate greenhouse panels

(3) 6-foot polycarbonate greenhouse panels

(2) 8-foot pieces of polycarbonate greenhouse H-channel

(4) Tubes of Lexel or clear silicon caulk

## Step One

Prep area next to house, making sure it is flat, well drained, and gets plenty of the southern sunlight.

## Step Two

Cut the base 4x4 timbers to length. Once the timbers are set in place and level, fasten each corner together with two 6 in. timber screws. Secure the frame to the ground by drilling holes through the frame and pounding 18–24" rebar stakes every 3–4 feet.

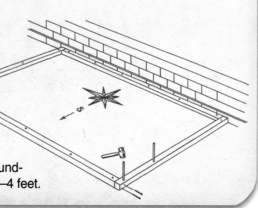

>>

**Tip:** This will make an 8x12 foot addition. You might want your man or a carpenter to do this project.

## Step Three

Cut the bottom plates, studs, and top plates to length. Assemble the wall, spacing studs every 48 inches on center. Drive four 3-inch deck screws through the top and bottom plates into the studs.

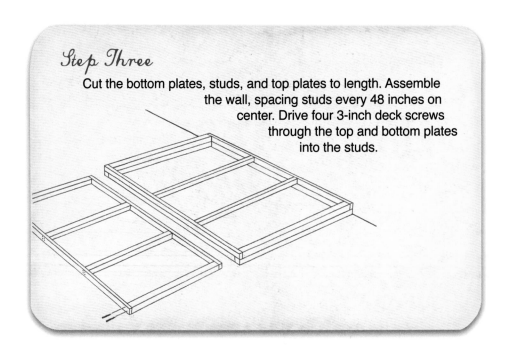

## Step Four

Raise the wall and fasten it flush to the timber base with 3-inch deck screws. Plumb and brace the wall.

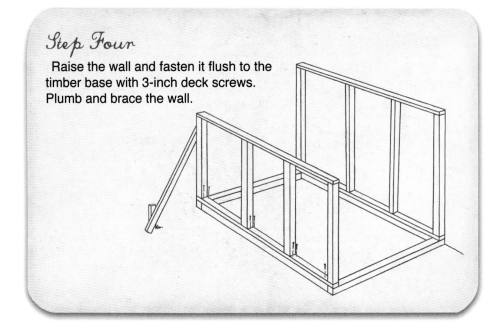

*Tip:* Having an access point to the house through the greenhouse makes for simple heating.

## Step Five

Make a template rafter with an 8-foot 2x4. Cut an 18-degree angle on one end, hold it to the peak of the roof, and scribe the bottom of the board to make your pattern.

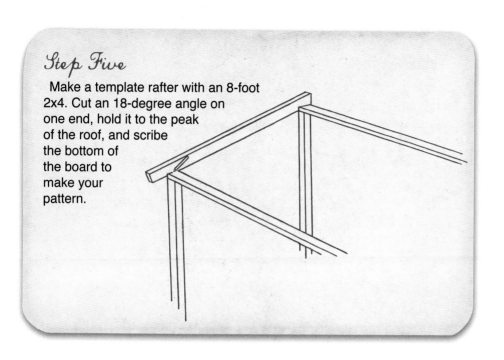

## Step Six

Measure, cut, and install 4x4 rafters with 6-inch timber screws. Install bird blocking and cross supports between rafters. (Be sure to countersink the screws so they do not stick up above the rafters.)

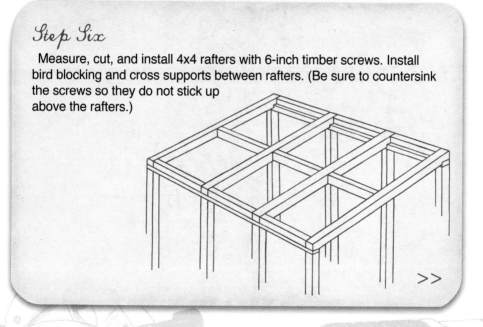

>>

## Step Seven

Measure, cut (with a sharp utility knife along a clamped straight edge), and install polycarbonate greenhouse roof panels using H-channel, U-trim, and 3-inch roofing screws. (Replace the roofing screw washers with larger washers from a greenhouse supply store. Also be sure to seal off all open roof panel cavities and install polycarbonate greenhouse U-trim on the top and bottom edges. Bugs love to crawl into the warm panels and lay eggs.)

## Step Eight

Make door to fit opening or get one from the hardware store before you start the project. It is best to have one with a large window.

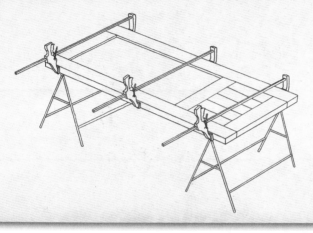

## Step Nine

Install roof or gable vent, or for a cheaper venting system, you can leave the door open and install one of the panels on the opposite side so that it can easily be removed.

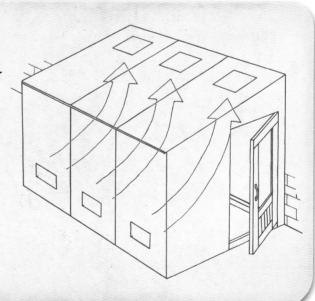

# *Rustic Table*

*I* grew up poor and loved making things out of nothing, and still do. This table is made from old barn boards that some guy was throwing out. We saw a collapsing barn on the side of the road and stopped and asked the owner if he wanted it cleaned up. We got a lot of old wood!

## Tools you will need:

1. Skill saw
2. Tape measure
3. Speed square
4. Framing square
5. Hammer
6. Carpenter's pencil
7. Cordless drill

## Materials you will need:

(10) 8-foot 2x4s, cedar

(4) 8-foot 1x10s, rough-cut oak sawmill lumber, or whatever hardwood they have. If you can't get sawmill lumber use deck boards from the hardware store or any old scrap lumber you can find.

(1) box outdoor deck screws (100–200 screws)

(1) ¼-pound 8D galvanized nails

| Key | Part | Qty. | Dimension | Material |
|---|---|---|---|---|
| A | Table Frame | 2 | 1½ x 3½ x 57" | 2 x 4 |
| B | Table Frame | 2 | 1½ x 3½ x 53" | 2 x 4 |
| C | Table Frame Leg Supports | 4 | 1½ x 3½ x 22" | 2 x 4 |
| D | Table Frame | 3 | 1½ x 3½ x 19" | 2 x 4 |
| E | Legs | 4 | 1½ x 3½ x 28" | 2 x 4 |
| F | Leg Supports | 1 | 1½ x 3½ x 55" | 2 x 4 |
| G | Table Top | 4 | ¾ x 9½ x 68" | 1 x 10 |

## Step One

Cut all boards to length, and fasten the table frame together with 3-inch outdoor deck screws.

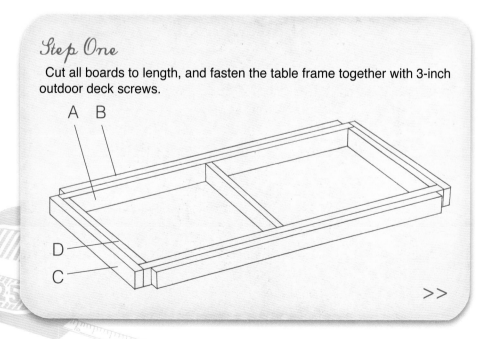

## Step Two

Attach the legs and cross brace with 3-inch outdoor deck screws, making sure the legs are square to the table frame.

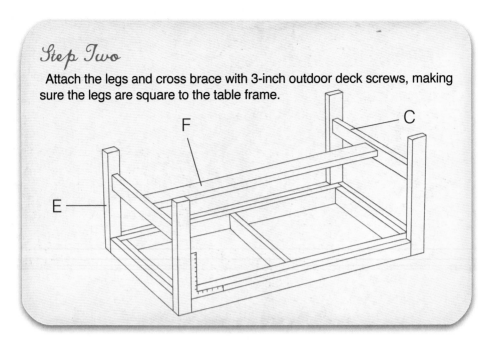

## Step Three

Turn the table frame 180 degrees on its legs. Cut boards for tabletop, allowing for approximately 2 inches of overhang, and attach the tabletop boards with galvanized nails.

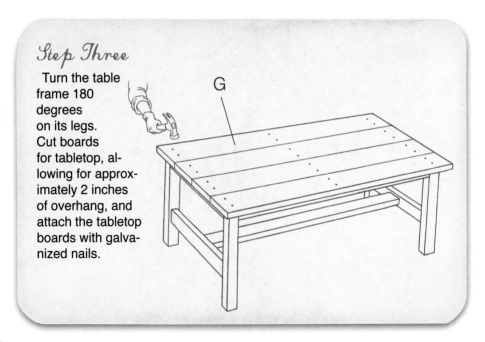

*Never miss a chance to dance, laugh or >> garden with your man!*

Easy *Garde* Box

*I* love the smell of fresh wood; not treated, painted, or stained, but fresh-cut grandpa style. Maybe it is because I grew up in the country or because we cut our own firewood, but I think there is nothing like it. I built my boxes out of rough-cut red cedar from our local mill. You can build them out of whatever you want, but cedar or other hard wood holds up best. If you want to garden in your backyard, then this is a great way to do it!

Look for a place that will get enough sun. If you live in a desert-like place, then it would need more shade. Factor in how much room you have and how much you want to plant. Then decide how big you want to build your boxes.

I built my beds 3 feet by 7 feet. I love them!

### Step One
Cut 4 boards 7 feet long, out of 2x12s .

### Step Two
Cut 4 boards 3 feet long, out of 2x12s.

### Step Three
Butt a 3-foot board against the end of a 7-footer, creating a L shape.

>>

*Tip:* Make sure you do not use pressure-treated wood. It is full of chemicals.

### Step Four

Screw four 2½-inch screws through the 7-footer and straight into the 3-footer.

### Step Five

Butt another 3-footer at the other end of the 7-footer, creating another wall for our rectangle.

### Step Six

Screw four 2½-inch screws through the 7-footer and straight into the second 3-footer.

### Step Seven

Use the second 7-footer to make the last side of a rectangle.

### Step Eight

Screw four 2½-inch screws through both ends of the 7-footer straight into the 3-footers.
You've got a raised bed!

*I*f you want a taller bed for longer-rooted things like carrots or potatoes, or just to be easier on your back, then build an identical box and attach it on top as follows:

*1.* Cut four boards that are 18 inches long.

*2.* Stack the two boxes and line them up.

*3.* Lay an 18-inch board flat on the ground and start 2 screws at the top and two screws at the bottom.

*4.* Center the pre-screwed board on an inside wall of your rectangular box; making sure it is lined up, screw all four screws in.

*5.* Repeat with the other 18-inch boards, one being used in the center of each side of the rectangle to stabilize the deep raised bed box.

*Tip:*

### Raised Bed Greenhouse
You can use the raised bed in the summer; add your cover before frost and keep your crop, or plant a new one. This is a great way to keep your cold crops growing all winter.

# Hillside Garden

I love my hillside garden. It started with carving away our driveway. We live on the side of a hill, and we have a circular driveway around our house. The bank was a time bomb of mud. Every time it rained, it would wash dirt down, and we would have a muddy mess and a smaller driveway. We carved our driveway wider with plans of pouring a footer and laying a block retaining wall. But looking at it a little closer, we knew that it would make the bank quite high. I was worried that one of our kiddos might climb up and fall off. That is when we came up with the hillside garden. We made three large, curved steps terracing up the hillside. We dug a footer along each step wall. We poured footers and laid blocks, enforcing with rebar and pouring every other one solid. We had a strong wall. After a few days of setting up, we backfilled. We added topsoil, compost, and manure. We used a rototiller to mix it all together, and covered it in wood chips. We had our hillside garden!

## Tools you will need:

1. Ground-marking paint
2. Tape measure

## People you will need:

1. Contractor with a track hoe
2. Block masons/concrete workers

## Materials you will need:

Enough rebar to strengthen your footer and perhaps stick up into the block wall

Enough concrete blocks to complete your wall project

Sand and mortar

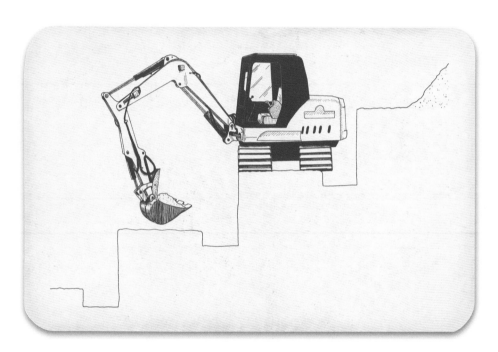

## Step One

Select hillside garden site, and with your contractor, mark out where you plan to dig. Excavate to create the proper ratio for each shelf, and dig 12 to 24-inch footers for walls. (Wider footers if you plan to have a curved wall.)

>>

 While excavating, dig away and pile up the good topsoil close by, so you can add it back to the terrace gardens.

## Step Two

Pour rebar-reinforced footers full of concrete, and lay up block walls and cap stones. (The wall can be poured solid for added strength. Also, taller walls may require drainage planning.)

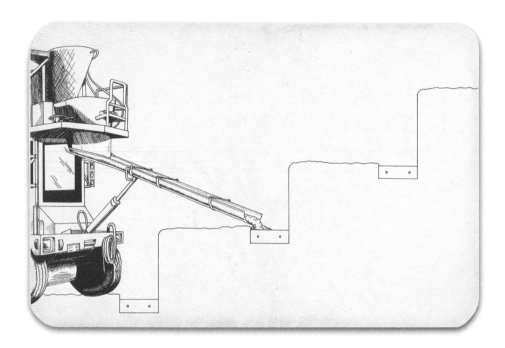

## Step Three

Backfill the terraces and layer in topsoil, composted manure, and woodchips. (We started our walls deeper than our finished grade level so that the footer would not limit our gardenable area.)

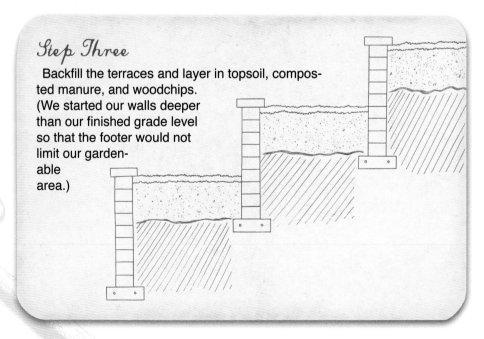

# Going Green

Playing house was a big part of my young life. My sister Shalom and I loved building playhouses out of everything left over from anything. We were like a Little Rascals playhouse-building army. We could whip one out every day. One year when Shalom was 11 and I was 9, Dad said our land was beginning to look like the landfill. He said we had to clean all but two of them up. That was a lot of cleaning! When I stopped to look around, I could see that our 25 playhouses resembled the landfill. But I liked the landfill—it was a great place to get playhouse supplies.

We started cleaning. It was fun going through and filtering the best stuff for our next playhouse. That winter, we had our job cut out for us. Cleaning them up definitely took longer than building them. So I began my search for a greener, more organic playhouse. I knew I wanted to add to my existing playhouse community, but without all the cleanup.

*"I looked straight up and determined that this was the perfect spot for my green, organic playhouse."*

Early that next spring, I was playing in the woods when I saw a bunch of small saplings (small trees)

growing close together. I got right in the middle of them and spread my arms out. There was a good four-foot space in the center of the bunch of trees. I looked straight up and determined that this was the perfect spot for my green, organic playhouse. I ran and got my sister Shalom to help me. We managed to get high enough to tie the sapling's tops together. We laid sticks up against the "walls" and then piled leaves all over it. We had a camouflaged, green, organic, self-cleaning playhouse. I was proud!

That summer we started making green bean teepees in our garden. That was cool! Not only were they clean and green, but you could sit inside and eat. Kids!

# Green Bean Bamboo Teepee

As a girl, I loved building green bean teepees. You can grow any vine you want on them, but climbing green beans are fun and easy, and they love growing on poles. They are great playhouses, and you never get hungry playing inside of them!

## Tools you will need:

1. Knife
2. Hand saw

## Materials you will need:

(1) 10-foot piece of garden twine

(10–15) 12-foot bamboo/cane poles

### Step One

Cut down bamboo/cane and place in a bundle with the largest ends even with each other. Approximately 8 feet up the poles, wrap the poles several times with the garden twine and tie with a secure knot.

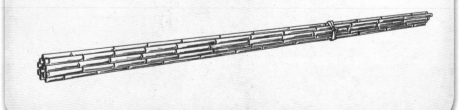

## Step Two

With two people, stand the poles up and pull the bottom ends out to make your teepee.

## Step Three

Plant your beans next to each pole and watch them grow and bear all season long.

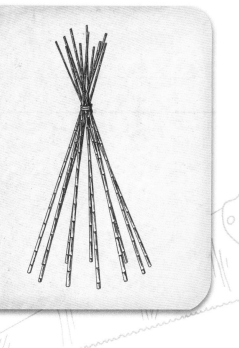

You can grow flowers, cucumbers, green beans, or a combination on this cool Indian teepee. It is a fun playhouse!

# Did You Know?

"Did you know . . . ?" That was something I heard every day growing up. I was homeschooled and my parents taught me with everything they did. Gardening, cooking, sewing, building—they were always talking us through the project. The more I learned, the more I realized I did not know, and that made me want to keep learning!

# Sustainable Gardening

Sustainable gardening is using an organic cover that breaks down and continually feeds your soil. This method will improve your soil every year. Gowing your vegetables in a sustainable gardening method will give you more delicious, nutritious, and all-around better vegetables. They are higher in vitamins, minerals, and nutrients. Sustainable gardening is known for its no-weed policy. I grew up on a farm and hoed thousands of weeds. That is a lot of sweat and hard work! Weeds always seemed to like the freshly plowed soil better than anything else. Now, I know that there are millions of tiny seeds lying dormant in the soil just waiting for some air and sun. There are around 140 seeds per pound of soil just waiting to grow. With every flip of the soil, more seeds are awak-

ened. Sustainable gardening gives a layer of mulch that keeps those seeds dormant.

Mulch also helps to hold in moisture, making for up to 95% less watering. The covering allows for less watering, but allows the soil to hold more moisture. Your fruits will have a higher brix and water content. Your plants will thrive when other gardens are dying.

Sustainable gardening is the perfect way to garden. It is agriculturally smart, not work intensive like most gardens, and you get a better vegetable. That is rewarding! I say, "Go organic, nutritious, and delicious!"

# Good Garden Soil

chalky soil *(bottom left)*, clay *(top right)*, good soil *(top left)*, sand *(bottom right)*

Good, organic soil is high in organic matter, holds moisture, allows the soil to breathe, and has a little compost to feed your plants. The soil should be the color of 70% dark chocolate. In one tablespoon of exceptionally healthy soil, there are over 20,000 living organisms.

If your soil is sandy, heavy in clay, or chalky, then you need to balance it. Add a lot of organic matter and compost. Cover it up with 4–6 inches of wood chips or your choice of organic mulch. Let it sit over the winter, and then you are ready to plant. The mulch will break down over the year, so add more in the fall as necessary. To add an extra boost, sprinkle some compost or rotted manure before applying mulch. In time your garden will be full of rich, nutritious soil.

# Building Healthy Soil

Think of it this way: your soil needs food, water, and skin. Give it what it needs and it will thrive.

Manure and compost are foods that feed the worms, which passively plow and fertilize your soil. Worm activity adds macro and micro-nutrients that help protect the soil from all kinds of disease, pests, and harmful bacteria and fungi. The soil needs water to activate the ingredients and encourage soil life; without it the nutrients will become inactive and stale.

Organic matter covering the soil is like the skin over your body. You need skin to protect you from the elements. The soil needs that protection too. Watch how the leaves fall in the forest and cover the forest floor. They are constantly breaking down and feeding the soil, protecting it from drying out and building a perfect home for all the soil's healthy critters. Check out *Making Vegetables Volume 3* for more extensive information on everything soil.

# Organic Matter

Organic matter is what remains of any organic, once-living material that has decomposed. When we use organic matter in the soil, we make sure it is free of any man-made chemicals. It will be dark in color and light in texture.

# Compost

Compost is alive. It contains a whole universe of microorganisms, good bacteria, fungi, and worms. Compost is made of materials full of nitrogen and carbon. Nitrogen (green stuff: manure, grass clippings, veggies, etc.) is the accelerant. It is what heats it up and starts the decomposing. Carbon (brown stuff: straw, dead leaves, wood chips, etc.) is the fuel that keeps the fire going. The microorganisms eat old veggies, manure, and scraps, and then poop it out as the perfect plant food. Good microbes need a balance of air, moisture, food, and organic matter. Not all composts are created equal. Check out *Making Vegetables Volume 3* for information on how to make perfect compost.

Jeremiah digging a hole in our wood chips to bury the kitchen scraps. Penelope Jane thinks he's cool!

# Jeremiah and the Compost

Every morning the kiddos make fresh, organic juice with their daddy. It is a great start to our day! Jeremiah goes to the root cellar and gets apples and carrots, then to the garden boxes to get greens, and then to the greenhouse to pick celery. He brings it in, and they all wash it. Then Penelope has to help with the juicing. They add a little of this and that and come out with something delicious. Then Jeremiah takes the scraps from the day before plus the veggie pulp outside, digs a hole in the wood chips, and buries it. Not only are we getting great enzymes to start our day, but we are also making humus that will grow more amazing veggies!

**Tip.** Check out *Making Vegetables Volume 3* to learn more about humus and composting.

This is the first and the last time I will ever rototill this garden. I am mixing up my ingredients, covering it with wood chips, and the worms will passively till it from here on out.

Less than one year after starting to build our soil, we have rich, dark soil, full of worms.

# Building Our Soil

When the dirt-moving guy was digging out our hillside for the garden area, we had him start by scraping the first 10 to 12 inches of topsoil up. That way we could use it in our garden when we finished the walls.

After the walls were done, we added our topsoil. Then we sprinkled equal parts compost and cow or horse manure on the top. We added hardwood ashes, which have lime in them and are good for the soil in our area. We sprinkled a little of our homemade fertilizer (pages 177-178) and sprayed it all with compost tea. We tilled it up and sprayed compost tea on it again. We let it sit for a few days, watering it a little every day. Then we planted it and laid 4 inches of wood chips over it. Eight months later in the cold of winter, I pull the wood chips back and reach my hand into the softest rich soil the color of 70% dark chocolate, full of worms. It smells alive—not stinky, but fresh. I am so excited to plant this spring!

## Beech Tree

When I was a girl, I would break a piece of mint off and plant it in a little pot. I would water it well, and it would grow roots within a few weeks. Then I would set up a stand and sell my mint plants for $1.25 each. I wanted to have no overhead for my little business, so I would go to the woods and dig soil out of a hollow beech tree. That way I did not have to buy it. It grew great plants! It looked rich and it was light and fluffy, so I knew it would work. Little did I know it was better than anything I could buy. It was organic humus!

# Humus

Good Garden Soil

Humus has the same ingredients as compost, but with less nitrogen. Less nitrogen keeps the pile from heating up like traditional compost, and allows it to decompose over a year, two, or longer. This provides longer, slower feeding of the soil through the year. Humus is also great for making compost tea. You can find it in nature. Check out *Making Vegetables Volume 3* and make it yourself, or see our Resources to buy it.

# Mulch

Mulch is a covering over the ground. It helps to hold moisture in and keeps the weeds from growing. It can be anything from plastic or cardboard to straw or wood chips. I prefer using organic mulch that will feed my soil while it decomposes. I have used all kinds of mulch including leaves, cardboard, plastic, straw, and hay, but my favorite is wood chips. Look in the woods. The trees drop leaves and sticks, and then old trees fall, slowly decomposing and becoming humus, which is the food that feeds the trees. When I was visiting the redwood forest I looked at the soil. It had a thick layer of mulch from the trees shedding. You could see and smell the rich soil. It was amazing! Mulch really works in the garden and in the wild!

You can sprinkle grass clippings on your wood chip mulch for plants that like nitrogen, but you want to make sure you are not adding seeds. Make sure that your grass clippings have not seeded.

I like to have a good 4 inches of mulch on my garden. You do not want to pile it on too thick because the soil needs to breathe.

You can get wood chips from tree trimming services. Having green matter, such as leaves, mixed with the brown is best. The green provides nitrogen and the wood, carbon. Together they decompose beautifully! Tree trimming services are normally looking for somewhere to drop off their chips. Ask around and you might be able to get them free right at your door. I live out in the country, so they do not like to drive all the way to my house. I go and pick them up free wherever they dump them. You can use a wide range of wood chips or other organic mulches, just like in nature.

# Good Garden Soil

# Manure, Manure, Manure

Plants love manure! It is high in nitrogen and makes leafy things thrive. Good microbes eat the manure and poop out plant nutrients. Not all poop is manure; some feces have pathogens and parasites that are harmful to humans. Not all manure is equal; it depends on what the animals eat and how they lived. The best manure would be from horses or cows that were grass fed, organically raised, or from poultry that were fed a non-GMO grain. Never put human, cat, or dog feces on your garden.

Too much green manure can burn your plants. Adding too much manure or any fertilizer can throw your soil off-balance. It is great to add, but you can add too much. If you are in a new garden spot trying to build up your soil, you might want to add ½ inch of green or composted manure over your soil, once or twice a year. If you have good soil, you might want to just add composted manure once a year. A good time to add it to your garden is in early or late winter. Some plants thrive with an extra helping of manure, and you can always add more composted manure to specific vegetables when you are planting.

You can get manure from local farms. Ask around and you might be able to find an organic or grass-feed farm. You can get a pickup-truck load for anywhere from 20–100 dollars. If it is composted manure, it will be a little more expensive. You can get it free if you are willing to muck out a stall. Just ask around at co-ops or wherever the farmers hang out.

Jeremiah James and Penelope Jane love gathering eggs! Eggshells are wonderful to compost too!

Shoveling composted
manure

You know what is in your fertilizer because you made it!

# Fertilizer

With soil that is low in minerals and nutritional plant food, plants will need fertilizer to be healthy. Germination and potting soil will only be good for short-term use due to their lack in plant food. You can sprout a seed in water but it needs nutrition for long-term growth. Most fertilizers consist of three main components: N–nitrogen, P–phosphorus, and K–potassium (NPK), along with some other important trace minerals such as calcium, magnesium, iron, copper, etc.

## Fertilizer Recipes

This one is an all-purpose fertilizer with balanced NPK.

4 parts alfalfa meal (Alfalfa is an herb full of vitamins and minerals. It is a great source of nitrogen but is also nicely balanced with phosphorus and potassium.)

¾ part high-calcium limestone (A biological sedimentary rock, high in calcium.)

¼ part gypsum (A sedimentary mineral. It helps to slowly soften the hard and clay-like soils.)

¾ part soft rock phosphate (A non-detrital sedimentary rock. Contains high amounts of phosphorous.)

¼ part bone meal (Optional. Can also just use 1 part soft rock. Bone meal is ground up bones. It has a good amount of phosphorous in it.)

1 to 2 parts kelp meal (A seaweed herb that is high in many trace minerals.)

This one is high in phosphorus and is great for root crops, like potatoes.

4 parts alfalfa meal

¾ part high-calcium limestone

¼ part gypsum

1 part soft rock phosphate

1 part bone meal

1 to 2 parts kelp meal

*Tip:* You can change this recipe to suit your soil needs, adding more or less of any ingredient or adding something new to it.

This one is high in nitrogen and is great for green tops, like lettuce.

5 parts alfalfa meal

½ part blood meal, an organic nitrogen fertilizer

¾ part high-calcium limestone

¼ part gypsum

¾ part soft rock phosphate

¼ part bone meal (Optional. Can also just use 1 part soft rock phosphate)

1 to 2 parts kelp meal

Have fun and create your own fertilizer to suit your needs!

### Applying Fertilizer

Spread about 1–2 cups of fertilizer per square foot on top of soil before planting. Using a hoe, mix into top 3 inches of soil. As a side dressing for established plants, apply ½–1 cup per plant, depending on the size of the plant, or 1–2 cups per foot of row. Apply according to your needs! Organic fertilizer rarely burns plants, so amounts are not set in stone.

Tip: After spreading fertilizer on soil, spray with compost tea before mixing it into the soil. This will help break it down faster and make it available to the plants.

James and Penelope
are making tea!

# Compost Tea

Compost tea is an amazing plant food. It is basically compost or humus mixed into water and aerated like an aquarium tank. This activates the live microbes in the compost and causes them to multiply rapidly. You can add organic fertilizer to the compost tea, and it will immediately start breaking it down and making it available for the plant. You spray it on the plants and soil, and it adds soil life and nutrients. Check out pages 31–35 to learn more about compost tea and how to make it.

*The fuzzy root means it is really healthy!*

## Good Bug, Bad Bug!

Good bugs pollinate your plants and kill bad bugs. You can squish and leave the bad bugs on your plants to deter other bad bugs.

# Pests & Disease

*Jeremiah holding a "good bug" — a lizard!*

Nature was made to heal and balance itself . . . if we let it. When a plant is sickly or lacking in nutrients, pests and disease can wipe it out. In the woods, a sickly tree will be eaten by beetles and fall over or die. The tree will decompose and feed the soil. Healthy soil will grow a healthy tree. The same holds true in the garden. If you start spraying chemicals, they will penetrate your soil and kill your soil life. You will have unhealthy soil long after the season is over. Your best defense against pests and disease is healthy soil.

So what about saving a crop that is already under attack? One great way is to use compost tea. It will strengthen your plants and act as an army of defense soldiers against pests and diseases.

If you have an infestation, say, on your eggplant, the first defense is finger squishing! Leave the dead bugs in the garden and it will help to keep the others away. Sometimes you just need an organic pest and disease spray to kill the little buggers. If so, these are some great recipes we came up with this year. You can change them to fit your needs.

## Notes:

Neem is an oil that is known for its anti-fungal properties. It is also anti-bacterial, and bugs hate it. Garlic and cayenne pepper are also anti-fungal and anti-bacterial and bugs hate them. Castile soap is a simple liquid soap; it is anti-fungal, antibacterial, and kills bugs when they come in contact with it. It will work only when it is wet, so spray in early morning or evening to avoid fast drying.

# Bug Spray

## Ingredients:

½ cup chopped cayenne peppers (or any hot peppers, the hotter the better)

3 to 4 cloves garlic, crushed

2 T. neem oil

1 T. liquid castile soap (either unscented or peppermint)

Enough water to make a gallon

*If you have a really bad infestation, you can double the peppers and garlic.*

## Step One

Place peppers and garlic in a blender, add water, and blend until smooth. Let sit for several hours or overnight to allow properties to be released into the water. Strain through a piece of muslin or old cloth. Pour in a gallon jar and add remaining ingredients.

## Step Two

Mix and spray on plants as needed. Try to spray only infested areas of your garden so that you don't kill all the beneficial insects. Make sure you cover both the tops and the undersides of leaves of infested plants. Can be applied every 7–10 days.

# Slug Away

To keep slugs away from your plants, put crumbled eggshells all around the base of your plant. The slugs will not want to crawl over the eggshells, and the eggshells will feed your soil!

Check out the pollen on that bumblebee's leg!

Dancing at the Heirloom Expo; Jeremiah learning from daddy!

# Seeds

# Heirlooms

Heirloom seeds have been saved from generation to generation. Many people ask, "How old does an heirloom seed need to be, to be called an heirloom?" Most people agree that after a seed has been saved for over 50 years, it is an heirloom. Heirlooms are also called heritage seeds.

They can be saved 50, 100, and even thousands of years. The fruit tastes much better than hybrid or genetically modified (GMO—more on hybrid and GMOs on pages 188-191) fruits. Heirloom seeds are known to produce fruits that are more delicious, nutritious, and colorful than other types of seeds.

Seeds

# Untainted Seeds

Ginseng was popular when I was an 8-year-old girl. It is great stuff and it grows wild in Tennessee. Everyone and their brother was hunting for it, and it was not easy to find. It takes seven years for a seed to grow and mature in the wild.

We wanted to make sure that we had it on our property for years and years to come. So my oldest brother Gabriel went out and found a few mature plants that had seeded. He got the seeds and planted them over my dad's 100 acres. I remember that it made a huge impact on me, that we were planting wild seeds in the wild. How cool was that?

The first time I heard of altered seeds, I was amazed. Why would anyone want to plant seeds that would produce seeds that are infertile or untrue to type? Why alter what God designed to be perfection? Heirloom seeds are simply using what God gave us—untainted seeds.

# Open Pollinated

Open pollinated seeds are basically hybrids that have been stabilized through growing, selecting, and saving the seed over many years. Every year it becomes more stable until eventually it will produce fruit that is true to type every time. These will be open pollinated (OP) seeds until they are about 50 years old. Then they will be called heirlooms.

# Hybrid

Most hybrid seeds are made with the pollen of two different species or varieties that have been genetically manipulated. They are called "hybrid F1" seeds. Hybridization can happen naturally too. Two tomato plants beside each other can cross-pollinate and produce a crossed tomato. If you plant that new seed, it will not be true to type, and it will be considerably less vigorous. You will not be able to plant it the following year because it is genetically unstable, and you never know what fruit it will bear. Hybrid seeds can be stabilized, becoming open-pollinated varieties, by growing, selecting, and saving the seed over many years.

# Squmpkin

*"Year after year I recall waiting and watching as her "pumpkins" would start to take shape and ripen"*

I have wonderful memories of helping my grandparents in their garden. My grandmother loved to save her seeds and plant them the next year. However, she never seemed to be able to produce a true pumpkin when she tried. Year after year I recall waiting and watching as her "pumpkins" would start to take shape and ripen. And year after year they kept ripening as a cross between a squash and a pumpkin. At the time, I had not realized that my frugal grandmother had planted her squash and pumpkins too close to each other. After so many years, they had crossbred into something entirely different. They still tasted good in a pie or some other well-seasoned dish, but their odd color and shape earned them the infamous name of "squmpkin," something that only grew in Grandmother's garden.

—James Easling

# GMO - Genetically Modified Organism

GMO stands for genetically modified organism. Scientists have taken DNA from plants and DNA from animals, mixed them together, and created a new seed. GMO seeds cannot be saved. They are infertile or do not grow true to type when you save and plant the seed. GMO foods are in almost everything we buy at the store: soy, corn, canola, and the list goes on. There is a lot of controversy over whether GMO foods are detrimental to our health. There is a fight to label foods that have GMO ingredients in them. Research on GMO crops is quite frightening. Check out the book *Seeds of Deception* by Jeffery Smith to learn more about GMOs.

The research that has been done on GMO vegetables is shockingly scary, but what is even more scary, is how little research has been done on these genetically altered vegetables.

# Heirloom Expo

Everyone was so friendly at the Heirloom Expo in Santa Rosa, California. We got to film and taste-test amazing heirlooms from all over the world. One place had apples. Oh, not the apples you buy in the store. These apples would turn your mouth inside out with flavor. I discovered taste buds I did not know I had. Mouth-watering, life-changing flavor! One apple was from a tree that was five hundred years old—amazing! My favorite was a red apple. When I say red, I mean the inside of the apple was red—wild! I am getting that seed! It was the best-tasting fruit I ever had!

Penelope
enjoying organic chocolate
ice cream at the heirloom expo

One of Papa Pearl's springs

*Water*

Water, water, water! Yes, there is more than one kind of water. In fact there are many kinds but we are going to talk about the main three kinds for watering your plants.

Rainwater and spring water are great! They will water your plants and feed your soil life. City water is another story. City water has been treated with chemicals that can diminish your plants' health and hurt your soil life. If you are working with city water, it is best to put it through a filter. If your city water is chlorinated, then you can let the water sit in a barrel for a few days, allowing the chlorine to dissipate. Try not to use water that has been through a softening system that uses salt—the salt will harm your plants.

## Old Timers

When you are looking for the right things to grow in your area, the best place to look is your area. Yes, you can talk to an heirloom seed specialist who can tell you what will grow in Alaska or Mexico, and that is great. But you can also ask the old-timers who have been saving seeds for years, and get seeds perfect for your area. The same seeds are not going to do well everywhere. A lot of old-timers are sad to let their seeds pass with their generation, and they are thrilled to give you a few to start your own collection.

## Last Frost

The date of the last frost is different from area to area. People like to plant after the last frost so their plants do not freeze. If you are in a colder area where the last frost is very late in the spring, or you just want an early harvest, then you might want to plant before the last frost and cover the plants with row cover to keep them from freezing. Here is a website that will help you figure out the last frost date for your area: www.almanac.com. Remember that these dates are approximate and you may want to wait a while longer to be safe.

"Tell him it's an annual, Mom!"

*Annual*
*Biennial*
*Perennial*

An *annual* is a plant that you plant every year. It grows, blooms, seeds, and dies in the same season.

A *biennial* is a plant that lives through two years. The first year it grows and the second year it matures, seeds, and dies. Onions and garlic are biennial.

*Perennials* are plants that come back year after year. A lot of herbs and flowers are perennials.

*Row*
*Cover*

Row cover can be as simple as throwing a sheet or fleece over your plants, or you can make a long-term row cover with wire arched and stuck into the ground, centered over the rows and covered in plastic or garden fleece (see Resources for garden fleece). When I was a girl, my mom used any old container, bucket, sheet, or piece of clothing to cover our plants. It looked like a mess, but it worked!

$\mathcal{F}$un and full of color, flavor, and variety, farmers' markets are the place to shop. You can ask around at your local health food store and find out where the nearest one is. There you will find fresh veggies picked that morning, as well as fresh breads, pastries, juices, fermentations, and so much more! It is a fun place to shop or have a booth. It is great to shop fresh and support your local economy.

*Jere, Emilee, and Sasha of Baker Creek*

# What the Experts Say

*I* feel so privileged to have been able to talk to and film so many experts on seeds, soil, composting, greenhouses, gardening, and preserving the harvest. These folks are the best at what they do. We learned so much that has changed our lives forever!

Jerit, our camera guy, and Penelope filming Shoshanna at the Heirloom Expo.

# Jere Gettle

Jere Gettle is the owner of Baker Creek Seed Company. He started the company fourteen years ago as a hobby and still loves it! As a family they grow, package, and sell old-time variety seeds. They want to get people back into growing their own food. Jere, his lovely wife Emilee, and their daughter Sasha live on a beautiful farm in Missouri. They have seed festivals with fun and educational days where you can learn more about heirloom seeds. Check out their website, *www.rareseeds.com*.

Here's what Jere has to say about seeds.

## Heirlooms

"An heirloom seed is a seed that has basically been passed down from generation to generation, and there's not really a set definition of how old it is. To different people, it's different things. It's kind of a loose term like antique or heritage, but in general it's something that's been in your family or families for generations."

## Hybrids

"Hybrid will grow any of numerous different combinations of types because it is not stable. The first generation of hybrids is what you plant when you get seeds at a grocery store, or so forth. But then, when you save seed from that seed you get into maybe 10 different types of tomatoes; you might get wild cherry tomatoes, you might get yellow tomatoes—you never know what you're going to get."

## Growing Heirlooms

"The biggest challenge with them, and it's also the biggest benefit, is you have varieties that come from hundreds of different countries. Literally every country on the globe has its heirloom varieties, and so you have a lot of diversity."

He goes on to say that if you live in Florida and plant all French heirlooms, then you might not have much luck because the climate in Florida is not the same as in France. Find heirlooms that suit your climate.

Some friends from Italy gave me some of their family heirloom seeds. They had moved to San Diego and their seeds were not growing the same as they did in Italy. Middle Tennessee's climate is similar to Italy's, so

I gave them a try. They were the best tomato seeds I have ever planted. I love them and they will be passed down though my family from generation to generation.

## GMOs

"GMO seed stands for genetically modified organism, which is basically a variety that is totally unnatural, nowhere found in nature. It is a variety that has genes inserted by scientists, by different seed companies or government agencies and so forth, that might have a flounder gene, or even human gene, genes from bacteria, or genes from other plants. These crops have unknown risks. They are also patented and controlled."

Once a year, Jere and Emilee Gettle of Baker Creek Heirloom Seeds have an heirloom seed and food festival called The National Heirloom Exposition in Santa Rosa, California. It is a spectacular event! People come from all over the world with heirloom seeds, knowledge, and their grandpa's wisdom. It is the information center of heirlooms, organic farming, and sustainable living.

Bakersville

**HOURS**
Mon.-Fri.
8 to 4
Sunday
9 to 5.
CLOSED SAT.

# Brad Gates

Brad Gates is the owner of Wild Boar Farms, where for fourteen years he has been breeding heirlooms of the future. He sells his tomatoes to restaurants, stands, farmers' markets, and customers who just drop by. We stopped by his beautiful farm and we were welcomed to walk around, take pictures, and pick fruit. Brad even let us have a tomato fight in his garden. Thanks, Brad!

"The reason I grow heirlooms instead of hybrids is, well, I've grown hundreds of varieties of each, and the reason my customers buy tomatoes is for flavor and nutrition, not for shelf life and appearance. That's why I grow 99% heirlooms."

"Can I taste the difference between a hybrid and an heirloom? Yeah, for sure! There are a few hybrids that I can say have a good flavor, or whatever, but I think the main incentive has probably been shelf life and appearance on hybridization. That's what the customers mainly have been wanting—eternal shelf life and beautiful appearance. It's kind of like the way they breed roses without the smell."

# William Weiss Weaver

William Weiss Weaver is from West Chester, Pennsylvania. He grew up with a big heirloom garden, saving and planting his own seed. He is now the author of sixteen books. His first book was *Heirloom Vegetable Gardening*, which helped to get the word *heirloom* more in the mainstream. When asked how many heirloom seeds were out there, this was his reply:

"I don't think anybody really knows, because first of all we have to define what is an heirloom. When you think there may be 6000 varieties of potatoes, and perhaps just as many varieties of tomatoes, and those are only two types of vegetables, and I can think of at least 300 or 400 different varieties of cabbage and maybe more. I'm sure we are talking about something in the vicinity of 200,000 or 300,000 food plants or more."

"I have a seed collection my grandfather started in 1930, that was my grandfather Weaver, and that whole story, by the way, is in my book *Heirloom Vegetable Gardening*. My own seed collection that I had built up after my grandfather died is about 4500 varieties of rare vegetables, many of which aren't found in any other seed collections. I made a point to collect things other people don't have, because I realize these seeds are rare and I've got to be Noah's ark a little

bit and help pass them on. I noticed here at the Heirloom Expo Fair there were some people selling the Fish Pepper. This was a pepper from my grandfather's collection that I sent seeds to Seed Savers Exchange, and now it's all over the place."

# Don Huber

Don Huber, emeritus professor of plant pathology at Purdue University, has spent 55 years researching biological disease control, microbial interaction, soil microbiology, bioterrorism, and food safety. Don is brilliant! He has done the research and knows the facts. He is so educated in the facts, it takes a minute to soak it all in. I love this interview because he is a scientist looking at the facts. It is really impacting. Check out the *Making Vegetables Volume 1* DVD for more of his interview.

"In that 55 years of research, I looked at microbial ecology, microbial interaction, involved with the soilborne diseases. I felt like I had a pretty good understanding of those interactions up until about 30 years ago, when we started seeing some changes. We saw our disease levels increasing, we saw our nutrient values decreasing, and because of the relationship between nutrition and disease, I started looking at those factors that have changed. In other words, when you start seeing a major change from what we've been seeing the previous 25 or 30 years, as a scientist you say, well, what has changed? And in looking at those changes, everything boiled down to the move to essentially a mono-herbicide, the glyphosate herbicide, and then in 1996 that was dramati-

cally impacted by the introduction of herbicide-tolerant crops, or Roundup-ready crops, where we saw the rate of glyphosate increase dramatically and saw its dramatic effect both on nutrition and nutrient availability, and the soil biology. Glyphosate is a very powerful antibiotic as well as a very potent herbicide."

"A GMO seed is a genetically modified seed or a genetically modified plant that has a foreign gene to produce a foreign protein. Genetic engineering is more like a virus infection, as Dr. Patrick Brown described it, than it is a normal breeding program. There is very little similarity between the genetic engineering process and the normal plant improvement enhancement process that's brought us all of our success,

*"There are tremendous health risks when you start producing many of these foreign proteins that are, in nature, only produced in bacteria or some other entity that we have little or no exposure to."*

yield, and quality improvement."

"There are tremendous health risks when you start producing many of these foreign proteins that are, in nature, only produced in bacteria or some other entity that we have little or no exposure to. When you start putting those proteins, those foreign proteins, directly into the food you're going to start eating, you have all kinds of potential. The other thing is that we know those proteins are extreme allergens, many of them very toxic to mammalian tissues, to humans. But the other thing is when you have this genetic engineering process, again it is very much like you would have with a virus infection. And you have all kinds of side effects; we call those epigenetic effects because we have inserted a gene and destroyed the integrity of the rest of the genetic code that is in that plant or that tissue, so that tissue then becomes very mutagenic. It starts producing and does produce many other compounds, most of those, compounds we've never looked at. We have no idea what they are and what their

toxicity is, what their safety is, or other effects that they would have, then, on the production of the plant or the safety of that plant. We know some of them are extremely toxic by themselves, so we have multiple toxins rather than just one."

"Heirloom seeds have a complete genetic complement. When you insert a gene through a normal breeding program, or change the genetics of a plant, you're transferring all the regulatory genes, control genes, all of the enhancing genes, to make that gene function in the plant only when the plant needs it. So it's not functioning all the time and it's not a burden on the plant. When we genetically engineer, again it's that virus-type infection and means the plant has to respond all of the time. It's just like your body responding to a foreign protein as an allergen or as a virus or a bacterium. It has to produce those anti-inflammatory compounds to try and defeat that foreign gene. You don't have that when you have a normal breeding program and a stable genetic code like you see with the heirloom seeds."

# Becky Schrock

Becky grew up Amish in Ohio where they did a lot of gardening. Now she runs her family's greenhouse where she starts seeds, grows seedlings, and sells her plants.

"Some potting soils are really heavy. You want to find something that is more light, spongy-kinda. It should be able to dry out but it also needs to be able to retain some moisture, because you do not want to be watering all the time.

When I start seeds I prefer planting them in small containers, just a couple of inches of soil. I just sow them in there, I do not plant them individually into the bigger pots. Then after they have grown to about their second leaf, I transplant them into the bigger containers. They seem to grow better and it is easier to keep the soil temperature and moisture even."

## Germination

"It's always good to keep your soil temperature as consistent as possible. Ideally it would be between 70° and 80°. Sometimes it's really hard to control that. I know for me, my greenhouse temperature has gone up to as high as 110 degrees for a little while, but you really don't want that to happen.

Also if it gets too cold for long periods of time, it may take them much longer for your seeds to come up, or they may never come out at all. You want to try and keep it between 70° and 80°. One way to keep the temperature up is to put your seed flats on heat mats. You can look for them online. They increase the soil temperature about 10° to 20° above room temperature."

## After Germination

"Seedlings stretch with too much heat.

You need to be careful; you might think heat is good, but too much heat is not good. It will make them grow faster and their strength will not be able to keep up with their height. They will get tall and skinny and have a hard time taking off when you transplant them.

Seedlings stretch without enough light.

It's really important for your plants to get enough light. If they don't they will stretch, or get tall and leggy, which is a condition that is almost impossible to correct."

## Watering

"You have to be very careful with watering. That is probably one of the biggest issues with seedlings. You want to make sure they do not dry out completely, because they do not have good root systems yet and they will starve quickly.

Overwatering is also a big problem. You want to make sure the soil dries out between waterings. They need to be moist all the way through but not soggy. Too wet will cause the seeds to rot. If they do get too wet then they will start falling over. Overwatering causes a disease called damping off, where the seedling rots at soil level. Damping off disease can also happen with poor ventilation."

## Growing

"After they are growing really well you can set them outside where the cold and the wind can get to them. They will love it! That will cause them to get strong and healthy, and it makes them just beautiful! Don't baby them too much. They have to get strong. Remember they are going to be out in the garden and they have to get prepared for that."

Becky was a huge help to the *Making Vegetables* series. She spent a lot of time in our garden.

# Dr. Patrick Vickers

Dr. Patrick Vickers is a researcher and chiropractor. He graduated from the University of Wisconsin and New York Chiropractic College. While he was a student at New York Chiropractic College, a woman by the name of Charlotte Gerson came and spoke at his school. Charlotte Gerson is the last living daughter of Dr. Max Gerson, the researcher who was reversing degenerative diseases, including terminal cancer. Dr. Patrick Vickers went on to study The Gerson Therapy.

"Can terminal cancer be cured? Absolutely it can! We have a 100-year history of reversing advanced terminal disease. Dr. Gerson was one of the most-published men in the world up until 1959, and his writings clearly proved that we can reverse terminal cancer. In fact, we are the only ones in medical history to have a peer-reviewed study proving the ability to reverse terminal cancer. It's called the Gerson Melanoma Study. We did our study on melanoma because it is the most aggressive cancer you can have. It is the most deadly cancer you can have, so we chose that one to do our study on. In that study we prove—no ifs, ands, or buts—we prove the ability to reverse advanced terminal cancer in 39% of those cases.

The reason why people have cancer today is because they are deficient. Not only are they overtoxic because of the things I mentioned in the environment, but they are deficient from 50, 60, 70 years of poor nutrition. Organic fruits and vegetables are absolutely vital for us to heal. The immune system functions on 59 different vitamins and minerals, and enzymes. And those enzymes, those vitamins, those minerals, not only do they go to destroy tumors and cancer cells, they are also responsible for rebuilding diseased tissue, rebuilding diseased cells, and breaking down diseased tissue. So fruits and vegetables are absolutely a vital source of nutrition for any cancer patient or any degenerative disease.

We cannot heal our patients without organic produce. Organic produce contains all the vitamins and minerals that are gained from

*" . . . conventional produce is grown with pesticides, herbicides, fungicides, all of which are deadly toxic with estrogens, heavy metals, which include mercury . . ."*

composted material. People who eat conventional produce simply cannot get the 59 essential vitamins and minerals necessary not only to maintain a proper immune system, a normal immune system, but certainly not a sick and dying one. Conventional produce is grown with three things: nitrogen, phosphorus, and potassium. That is the standard artificial fertilizer that farmers are using today. It's called NPK. Farmers and scientists have figured out that they can grow big, beautiful vegetables using those three chemicals. The problem is, like I said, the immune system requires 59 other vitamins and minerals to be healed. So artificial and conventional produce simply cannot heal a sick and dying patient. The other things regarding conventional versus organic—the obvious one—is that conventional produce is grown with pesticides, herbicides, fungicides, all of which are deadly toxic with estrogens, heavy metals, which include mercury . . . a lot of your tomatoes and strawberries are laced with mercury-laden and petroleum-based pesticides. So that's the obvious reasons. We are trying to detoxify a body, not intoxicate it.

One thing people don't understand about conventional produce is that before it goes to market they irradiate it, and the reason why they irradiate it is because when you irradiate something you kill off enzyme activity. When you kill off enzyme activity, you can store it for longer. It won't go bad as quickly, so stores will have it irradiated before it goes to market so they can preserve their profits, so they do not have to throw away produce so quickly. The problem with that is enzymes are vital. Enzymes kill cancer cells. Enzymes literally dissolve tumors. They literally rebuild and break down diseased tissue, so without those enzymes we simply cannot heal. Now organic laws in the United States today clearly state you cannot irradiate produce. Those laws might change in the future, but as of right now, true organic produce that you buy at the markets cannot be irradiated."

*Making fresh juice!*

# Recipes

*Y*UM! I love good food! My son Jeremiah James always says, "Food needs to be healthy and delicious!" I agree! It all starts with the ingredients. Growing your own organic, nutritionally dense heirloom vegetables and letting them shine is the key.

# Baked Kohlrabi Tacos

### Prep: 7 min.  Cook: 10-12 min.  Serves: 4-6

*I* love these! They are like a fish taco, but with even more flavor. This is a great main dish and also makes for a really fun appetizer.

2 kohlrabi, peeled and sliced ½-inch thick

1 Tbsp. butter, plus more for buttering pan

1½ tsp. ground cumin

1½–2 tsp. sea salt

½ tsp. black pepper, freshly ground

Zest and juice of ½ lemon

1 avocado, mashed

1½ tsp. sea salt

1 cup mung bean sprouts, rinsed

1 cup very thinly sliced radishes

1 cup cilantro, chopped

2 Tbsp. chopped mint

2 lime wedges

6 to 8 corn tortillas

### Step One

Preheat oven to 475°. Place kohlrabi slices in a single layer on a buttered baking pan.

### Step Two

Spread 1 T. butter equally on tops. Sprinkle with salt, pepper, cumin, and lemon zest. Squeeze lemon juice on top and bake on top shelf for 10–12 minutes or until desired tenderness.

### Step Three

Mash avocado and mix with salt.

### Step Four

Rinse mung bean sprouts.

### Step Five

Wash and thinly slice radishes.

### Step Six

Wash and chop cilantro and mint.

### Step Seven

Wash and wedge limes.

### Step Eight

Heat corn tortillas in buttered skillet.

### Step Nine

Place baked kohlrabi on tortilla, layer with rest of ingredients as toppings, squeezing fresh lime juice on top. Delicious!

*Tip:* You can eat kohlrabi so many different ways. Try peeling, chopping, lightly boiling it in water, and then adding butter, salt, and pepper. YUM!

Purple heirloom kohlrabi
that we grew in our
greenhouse this past winter

# Cheesy Veggie Rolls

Prep: 8 min.  Chill: 1 hour  Serves: 6

My kiddos love when I make these! They are a fun and easy afternoon snack with a good mix of creamy cheese and the crunch of the fresh broccoli and toasted nuts.

1¾ cup fresh broccoli

¼ cup chives

¼ cup parsley

1 8-ounce block of cream cheese (room temperature)

½ cup sour cream

1 cup white cheddar cheese

½ to ¾ tsp. sea salt

1 tsp. onion powder

½ cup pine nuts or chopped pecans, toasted

2 to 3 large tortillas

### Step One
Wash and finely chop broccoli.

### Step Two
Wash and chop parsley and chives.

### Step Three

Whip cream cheese and remaining ingredients except tortillas with electric mixer.

### Step Four

Put 1 large spoonful of cheese mixture on tortilla.

### Step Five

Spread mixture over tortilla.

### Step Six

Roll tortilla up.

### Step Seven

Chill wraps in refrigerator for one hour and then slice.

# Garden Eggs Benedict

Prep: 8 minutes   Cook: 15 minutes   Serves: 6

Poached eggs can be intimidating but they do not need to be. With these steps and a little practice, you will be making them for the whole family. They are so delicious! My whole family loves when I make this for breakfast!

## Hollandaise Sauce:

¼ cup dry white wine

1 Tbsp. white wine vinegar

1 Tbsp. minced shallots

½ tsp. cracked black peppercorns

3 Tbsp. boiling water

3 large eggs

¾ cup butter, at room temperature

1 tsp. fresh lemon juice

½ tsp. sea salt

a good pinch of cayenne pepper

## Blanched Asparagus:

Large handful of fresh asparagus

Water for the pan

Sea salt to taste

## Poached Eggs:

6 to 8 eggs

1 Tbsp. white vinegar

Water for pan

## Hollandaise Sauce:

### Step One

In a saucepan combine wine, vinegar, shallot, and peppercorns. Cook over medium-high heat 3 to 4 minutes, until liquid has reduced to about 1 tablespoon. Add boiling water to shallot mixture and strain through a sieve into a heat-proof, nonreactive bowl (glass or stainless).

## Step Two

Separate egg yolks from whites (egg whites will not be needed). Beat egg yolks until light in color, then mix into strained reduction. Gently place bowl of egg yolk mixture into the saucepan of simmering water. Whisk constantly until mixture thickens enough to hold a trail. (Tip: If the egg yolks are cooked too quickly they will become grainy, if they are cooked too long or on high temperatures, they will scramble.)

## Step Three

Remove from heat and whisk in 1 tablespoon butter at a time, whisking well before you add the next tablespoon. Add lemon juice, sea salt, and cayenne. Your sauce should be thick but still able to drizzle. If it mounds, then it's too thick and you need to add a little water.

## Asparagus:

### Step One

Wash and cut off tough ends of asparagus. Bring an inch of water to boil in a saucepan, then turn down to light simmer and drop asparagus in. Cover with a lid for 1 to 2 minutes, then remove lid and flip asparagus. Cover with lid for another minute and the asparagus should be ready. It is best lightly cooked, still very green, with a nice, crisp bite. Drain and keep warm.

## Poached Eggs:

### Step One

In a deep saucepan, add a tablespoon of vinegar to 2 inches of water. Bring to a boil and then turn down to medium heat. Water should be barely simmering.

### Step Two

Crack egg in a small bowl and gently immerse halfway underwater, slowly pouring egg in a fluid motion into water. As soon as egg is in the water, use a spoon to fold any stray egg whites over egg to create a nice egg ball. Cook until whites are set but the center is soft and still runny. Two or three minutes is enough. Don't overcook!

### Step Three

Gently lift egg out with a slotted spoon or small mesh sieve. Trim egg white pieces to make a clean, pretty presentation.

### Assembly

Lay asparagus on a plate, top with egg and hollandaise sauce. You can also add an extra dash of cayenne on top. YUM! Enjoy!

**Tips:**

- Use fresh eggs.
- Keep water barely at a simmer but not boiling. If the water is moving you will have a messy egg.
- You can cook 4 at a time, but make sure you watch them well and don't let them overcook.

# Spring Pizza

Prep: 20 min.  Rise: 1 hour
Cook: 7 min.  Serves: 6

*T*here is so much to say about this amazing pizza! Slightly chewy crust with fresh garlic, olive oil, veggies, herbs, cheese, and arugula—it is simply scrumptious!

1 cup warm water

1 tsp. honey

2 tsp. active dry yeast

2¼ cups whole wheat flour + a little for kneading

1¼ tsp. sea salt

Olive oil for rubbing on dough

6–7 cloves garlic (about 3½ Tbsp. crushed)

5 Tbsp. olive oil

1–2 leeks, rinsed and chopped (about 1½ cups)

½ tsp. sea salt

6 oz. cream cheese

10–12 mozzarella balls, pulled apart into small pieces

2–3 radishes, thinly sliced

2–3 green onions, chopped

¾ cup arugula, coarsley chopped

4 Tbsp. chopped cilantro

## Step One

In a bowl, dissolve honey in warm water. Add yeast and stir. Cover and let sit in a warm spot for 5 to 7 minutes or until frothy.

## Step Two

Add half of the flour and mix on medium-low for 3 minutes. Slowly mix and gradually add the rest of the flour and 1¼ teaspoons sea salt.

## Step Three

Pour dough out on floured surface and knead for 5 minutes.

## Step Four

Roll dough into a ball, rub a little oil over it, and put it in a bowl. Poke holes in it, cover, and let it sit in a warm spot. Let it rise for 45 minutes to 1 hour or until dough doubles.

## Step Five

Punch dough down and knead for 1 minute.

## Step Six

Pinch dough into 2 pieces.

## Step Seven

Roll each piece into a ball. Lightly rub them with oil and let sit in a warm area for 15 minutes.

## Step Eight

Preheat oven to 475°. Sprinkle corn meal on cookie sheet or pizza stone; if using a stone, preheat it first.

## Step Nine

Punch down, knead, and roll crust out to ¼-inch or thinner. Fold dough like a napkin to move to baking pan.

## Step Ten

Unfold dough on pan and stretch out.

### Step Eleven

Use a fork and poke 10 to 15 times into the crust. Bake crust for 3 to 5 minutes, depending on thickness.

### Step Twelve

Prepare garlic confit: crush 2½ Tbsp. garlic cloves, add 4 Tbsp. olive oil, and set aside.

### Step Thirteen

Sauté leeks in 1 Tbsp. olive oil over medium heat until soft and lightly browned. Add salt to taste.

### Step Fourteen

Brush garlic confit on golden brown pizza crust.

### Step Fifteen

Layer on leeks, cream cheese droplets, and pulled-apart mozzarella.

## Step Sixteen

If your pizza is on a cookie sheet, slide it off the sheet directly onto the oven rack so the crust will get crisp. Return to oven for about 1 to 2 minutes until crust has a nice crunch and cheese is melted.

## Step Seventeen

Layer radish slices, green onions, arugula, and cilantro on top of hot pizza. Serve immediately!

# Strawberry Pancakes

Prep: 12 min.  Cook: 12 min.  Serves: 4-6

*S*pring brings delicious things! Fresh strawberry pancakes are a must with spring in the air. These pancakes have a nice nutty taste with a hint of citrus. Jeremiah and Penelope love helping me make pancakes in all kinds of shapes. They love making them almost as much as eating them—almost!

⅓ cup pecan meal

½ cup almond meal

1 cup gluten-free flour mix

1 tsp. sea salt

½ tsp. baking soda

1½ tsp. baking powder

1 cup milk or nut milk

2 eggs

1½ tsp. vanilla

2 tsp. coconut oil, melted

1 Tbsp. honey

1 lemon

8–10 strawberries

### Step One

Zest one lemon.

### Step Two

Mix first six ingredients and 1 teaspoon lemon zest.

### Step Three

In another bowl, mix the next 5 ingredients.

### Step Four

Mix dry and wet ingredients together to make batter.

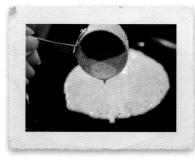

### Step Five

Heat and grease flat iron or griddle to medium-low and pour on ⅓ cup pancake batter.

## Step Six

Cook until you see little bubbles coming through your pancake.

## Step Seven

Flip cake and cook until golden brown.

## Step Eight

Wash and slice strawberries.

## Step Nine

Top pancakes with strawberries, lemon zest, and real maple syrup to desired taste.

Fruits and veggies are highest in flavor and nutrition the day you pick them, so pick your strawberries fresh!

# Asparagus with White Cheese Sauce

Prep: 15 min.   Cook: 10 min.   Serves: 4

Spring asparagus, fresh and tender—yum! There is so much you can do with asparagus from breakfast to supper. Fresh with dip, steamed with cheese, baked in quiche—the possibilities are delicious! The first time I was introduced to asparagus it was steamed with cheese, and I have been hooked ever since. Asparagus is so good for you. In fact, it is a fertility food. Off point maybe, but it is true!

2 handfuls fresh asparagus

½ tsp. lemon zest

½ tsp. sea salt

⅛ cup butter

1½ Tbsp. flour

½ tsp. sea salt

¼ tsp. nutmeg

⅛ tsp. onion powder

Dash of black or cayenne pepper

1 cup milk

¼ cup freshly grated Parmesan cheese

½ cup freshly grated white cheddar cheese

### Step One

Wash and chop any tough ends off asparagus.

### Step Two

Put 1 inch of water in large pan and bring to boil. Drop asparagus in water and cook for 1½ to 2 minutes.

### Step Three

Remove asparagus from water.

### Step Four

Sprinkle lemon zest and sea salt over asparagus.

*Tip*: Don't overcook! Asparagus is great fresh and really only needs a light blanching when it is cooked.

## Step Five

Melt butter in saucepan; add flour and seasonings. Stir until well blended, and cook on medium heat for 1 minute.

## Step Six

Add milk gradually, stirring constantly. Bring to a boil and simmer for 2 minutes.

## Step Seven

Remove from heat and stir in grated cheese.

## Step Eight

Pour cheese sauce over asparagus and serve!

Tip:
If you want to change up your white sauce, use another kind of white cheese or add a few tablespoons of white wine to it.

# Brie and Veggies

Prep: 12 min.  Serves: 4-6

6 thin slices of bread
⅓ to ½ cup brie (cheese)
1 fresh large radish
3 fresh peas
1 to 1½ tsp. lemon zest
1 tsp. fresh herbs, such as
  chives, mint, or parsley
  (optional)

*I* could eat this every day! Brie is a tart, rich, creamy cheese that works perfectly with the sweet crunch of fresh peas. I prefer using a chewy, light, airy bread with this recipe so as not to weigh down the lightness of all the flavors. This is a wonderful, crowd-pleasing finger food or a delectable afternoon snack!

### Step One

Slice and lightly toast bread.

### Step Two

Wash and thinly slice radishes and peas.

### Step Three
Wash and chop herbs.

### Step Four
Wash and zest lemon.

### Step Five
Spread brie over toast and sprinkle veggies and herbs on top.

# Curried Cauliflower

Prep: 5 min.   Cook: 15 min.   Serves: 4-6

*𝒯his is so good! I gave this cauliflower a Thai spin. Penelope was helping me make it and she kept snitching pieces—it's that good!*

2 medium-size cauliflower heads, about 6 cups florets

4 Tbsp. coconut oil

4 cloves garlic

¼ tsp. pepper, freshly ground

1 tsp. sea salt

1 tsp. ground cumin

½ tsp. ground coriander seed

1 tsp. curry powder

2 tsp. lime zest

2 tsp. lime juice

1 tsp. freshly ground ginger

2 Tbsp. chopped cilantro

3 Tbsp. pine nuts or slivered almonds, dry roasted

### Step One

Cut cauliflower into medium-size florets

### Step Two

Place cauliflower in a single layer on sheet pan

### Step Three

Peel and slice garlic, and toss on top of cauliflower.

### Step Four

Melt coconut oil and drizzle 2 tablespoons over the cauliflower.

### Step Five

Sprinkle with sea salt and pepper.

### Step Six

Roast for 10 to 15 minutes at 400°, turning every 5 minutes until cauliflower is firm but tender, and some of the tips are browned.

### Step Seven

Remove cauliflower from oven and immediately sprinkle with cumin, coriander, and curry powder; toss together.

### Step Eight

Combine zest, lime juice, ginger, and remaining 2 tablespoons coconut oil. Drizzle over cauliflower.

## Step Nine

Roast nuts in small pan over medium heat until lightly toasted.

## Step Ten

Add nuts and cilantro to cauliflower. Toss and serve hot!

# Fresh Pickled Beets

Prep: 7 min.    Serves: 4-6

2 small beets
1 cup water
1 tsp. honey
1 tsp. parsley
⅓ cup vinegar
½ tsp. sea salt
1 tsp. lemon zest

When I was a girl my mom always made our cucumbers like this. I loved them! We ate them almost every day in the summer. I love making beets like this because it gives them a really great pickled flavor!

### Step One

Wash, peel, and slice beets.

### Step Two

Mix vinegar, water, salt, honey, parsley, and lemon zest together and drop in beets. Let sit for 15 minutes before serving.

# New Potatoes

Prep: 8 min.   Cook: 20 min.   Serves: 6-8

*A*s a child I would wiggle my bare feet into the soil as my daddy dug new potatoes. I would pick them up and put them in our bucket, and then help my mama wash and cook them. They were delicious just like these!

15 new potatoes

1 tsp. lemon juice

1 Tbsp. butter

1½ tsp. sea salt

2 Tbsp. lemon zest

½ tsp. ground pepper

2 Tbsp. thyme

*Step One*

Wash potatoes.

*Step Two*

Add potatoes to pan with ½ inch water and steam until soft, about 20 minutes.

*Step Three*

Add butter, lemon zest, thyme, and pepper.

*Step Four*

Gently mix in and serve.

# Papa Glen's Potatoes

Prep: 12 min.  Cook: 55 min.
Serves: 6-8

8–10 potatoes
½ large onion
1½–2 tsp. salt
5 Tbsp. butter
1 tsp. pepper, freshly ground
2 Tbsp. fresh parsley, chopped

*P*apa Glen was known for fishing and cooking great food. He was the best grandfather a girl could ask for. He loved teaching me how to cook. I remember when he taught me how to make these potatoes. Delicious and fun!

### Step One

Wash and slice potatoes.

### Step Two

Peel and slice onions.

### Step Three

Layer potatoes, onions, butter, salt, and pepper.

### Step Four

Put in 8x8-inch or somewhat larger baking dish and cover with a lid or foil.

### Step Five

Bake at 350° for 50 minutes, or until soft.

### Step Six

Carefully remove cover, and broil for 3–5 minutes or until lightly toasted.

### Step Seven

Sprinkle fresh parsley on top and serve.

When I was a girl I ate beets because I thought they were a pretty color. Now I eat them because I can make them delicous!

# Steamed Beets

2 beets
½ tsp. lemon zest
1½ tsp. butter
½ tsp. lemon juice
1 tsp. fresh parsley,
   chopped
⅓ tsp. sea salt

Prep: 8 min.   Cook: 5 min.   Serves: 4

### Step One

Wash, peel, and chop beets.

### Step Two

Put in pan with ½ inch water. Cover and cook for five minutes.

### Step Three

Remove from heat and mix in remaining ingredients.

# Brussels Sprout Shred

Prep: 8 min.   Cook: 1-2 min.   Serves: 2-3

10 Brussels sprouts
2 Tbsp. butter
Dash cayenne
½ tsp. sea salt
½ tsp. lemon zest

### Step One

Wash and grate brussels sprouts.

### Step Two

Heat butter in pan on medium-high until hot. Add brussels sprouts and cook 1-2 minutes, turning so they do not burn.

### Step Three

Remove from heat. Add salt, cayenne, and lemon zest. Serve hot.

*J*ames and I love going out to wonderful restaurants and tasting new ways of cooking vegetables. That is where I got this amazing idea! Yum!

# Granny's Slaw

Prep: 15 min.    Serves: 6-8

1 cup carrots
5 cups cabbage
½ cup Vegenaise or
    mayonnaise
3 Tbsp. vinegar
2 tsp. salt
1 Tbsp. honey
1 tsp. pepper

## Step One

Grate cabbage and carrots.

## Step Two

Mix remaining ingredients in a bowl.

## Step Three

Pour dressing over slaw and mix.

_Granny taught me how to make slaw. It is great on sandwiches or as a side! The perfect tartness!_

# Kohlrabi Salad

Prep: 15 min.   Serves: 4-6

*K*ohlrabi is one of those vegetables that most people pass up because they do not know what they are missing! It is sweet, crunchy, and great fresh or cooked!

2⅔ cups kohlrabi, cut in small cubes

1 Tbsp. chopped mint

1 Tbsp. chopped basil

1 Tbsp. lime juice

2 Tbsp. Vegenaise or mayonnaise

1 tsp. (or a little more) lime zest

½ tsp. honey

¼ tsp. sea salt

## Step One

Wash and chop herbs.

### Step Two

Wash and zest lime.

### Step Three

Mix herbs, Vegenaise, honey, salt, zest, and juice together.

### Step Four

Wash, peel, and chop small cubes of kohlrabi.

### Step Five

Poor dressing over kohlrabi and toss. Enjoy!

**Tip:** You can change this recipe by using lemon instead of lime, and parsley instead of one of the other herbs.

# Papa Glen's Salad

Prep: 15 min.    Serves: 6

Papa Glen knew how to make a good supper! This salad was almost always on the menu. It was always made fresh.

¾ cup vinegar

½ cup olive oil

1½–2 tsp. oregano

¾ tsp. whole peppercorns

1 clove garlic

½ tsp. salt

1 tsp. honey

10 cups mix of romaine, baby kale, baby spinach, and other hardy greens

½ cup or more fresh bacon bits

2 sliced, hard boiled eggs

2 thin slices purple or red onion

## Step One

Cut and wash greens.

## Step Two

Blend vinegar, oil, oregano, peppercorns, garlic, salt, and honey in a blender until smooth.

## Step Three

Slice eggs and onion.

## Step Four

Add eggs, onion, and bacon bits to greens.

## Step Five

Pour dressing over and toss salad. Serve immediately.

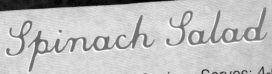

# Spinach Salad

Prep: 8 min.    Cook: 3 min.    Serves: 4-6

This is a rich salad with a lot of flavor! Sometimes I use blue cheese instead of feta. That makes it really rich!

| | |
|---|---|
| 8 cups spinach | 1½ tsp. sea salt |
| 1 small garlic clove, crushed | ½ cup sunflower seeds |
| ⅛ cup olive or grapeseed oil | 1 tsp. butter |
| 1 tsp. maple syrup | ¼ cup tart red cherries or cranberries |
| 1 dash cayenne | |
| ½ tsp. lemon zest | ¼ cup feta cheese |

## Step One

Cut and wash spinach.

## Step Two

Mix next 5 ingredients and 1 teaspoon sea salt to make dressing.

## Step Three

Toast sunflower seeds by rubbing them with butter and ½ teaspoon sea salt and toast in a pan over medium heat for three minutes or until golden-brown.

## Step Four

Pour dressing on spinach.

## Step Five

Top with toasted sunflower seeds, cranberries, and feta.

# Strawberry Pecan Salad

Prep: 15 min.  Cook: 3 min.   Serves: 8

*T*his is one of my favorite salads! I love the dressing on this. It has a nice tart and sweet flavor! My kids love it too!

6 strawberries

24 peas

⅓ cup parsley, chopped

16 cups arugula and other lettuce greens, washed

½ cup pecans

1 tsp. butter

½ tsp. salt

Small pinch of cayenne

## Step One

Rub pecans with butter and salt. Broil in oven for three minutes, or toast them in a pan on stovetop. Toasted pecans should be golden-brown.

## Step Two

Wash strawberries and peas.

## Step Three

Slice strawberries.

## Step Four

Blend lemon juice, lemon zest, honey, grapeseed oil, and salt.

## Step Five

Add pecans, strawberries, and parsley to greens.

## Step Six

Pour dressing over salad and toss.

# Thai Salad

Prep: 12 min.    Serves: 8

*J*ust before I married James, I was in Thailand on a mission trip. I loved hanging out with the locals. I taught them how to make pancakes and they taught me how to cook Thai and Lao food. They use so many fresh herbs in their cooking. One thing I thought was funny is that they use cabbage in place of lettuce for all of their salads. A lot of my cooking inspiration comes from them. This is a delicious salad with the flavors of Thailand and Laos.

¾ head green cabbage (about 6 cups shredded)

⅓ head purple cabbage (about 3 cups shredded)

2 green onions

¾ cup cilantro

1 cup feathered carrots

3 radishes (about ½ cup sliced)

2 Tbsp. mint, chopped

¼ cup Vegenaise

¼ cup olive oil

1 tsp. cumin

½ tsp. pepper

1½ tsp. salt

1 Tbsp. maple syrup

Small dash cayenne

### Step One

Thinly chop cabbage.

### Step Two

Wash and chop green onions, mint, and cilantro.

### Step Three

Thinly slice radishes and feather carrots.

### Step Four

Toss first 8 ingredients together.

### Step Five

Mix remaining ingredients together to create dressing. Pour over salad, toss, and serve.

# Cornmeal Shortcake with Strawberries and Cream

Prep: 35 min.  Cook: 18-20 min.  Serves: 6-8

*A* few years ago at our church we had a field-corn contest. My dad grew a lot of field corn and brought some extra to church to give away. For our fall fest we all came to church with our best corn recipes. There were about 100 dishes from corn ice cream to corn bread. I worked like a mad scientist coming up with the best desserts corn could make. It was so much fun that I still love adding it to things you would not expect it to be in. I created this shortcake recipe last year, and it is amazing!

1 cup unbleached white flour

½ cup yellow cornmeal

2¼ tsp. baking powder

¾ tsp. sea salt

½ cup sugar

4 Tbsp. cold butter

½ cup milk

½ tsp. vanilla

2½ tsp. orange zest

1 quart fresh strawberries

1½ cups heavy whipping cream

½ tsp. vanilla

¼ cup powdered sugar

## Cornmeal Shortcake:

### Step One

Take out ½ tablespoon sugar and set aside, and then mix first five ingredients.

### Step Two

Cut cold butter into dry ingredients.

### Step Three

Mix milk, vanilla, and 1 teaspoon orange zest into dry ingredients.

### Step Four

Grease baking sheet and sprinkle with cornmeal.

### Step Five

Drop dough in large spoonfuls on sheet.

## Step Six

Sprinkle with the reserved ½ table-spoon sugar and the rest of the orange zest.

## Step Seven

Bake on bottom rack at 350° for 18 to 20 minutes or until golden. Meanwhile, prepare strawberries and cream.

## Strawberries and Cream:

## Step One

Wash and slice strawberries.

## Step Two

Using a potato masher, mash straw-berries and set aside.

## Step Three

Whip heavy cream with electric mixer on medium-low until soft peaks form.

## Step Four

Add vanilla and powdered sugar and whip until combined (about 10 seconds).

*Assembly:*

## Step One

When cakes are finished, take out and let cool for 10 minutes.

## Step Two

Gently cut cakes in horizontal halves.

## Step Three

Layer cake, cream, and strawberries, top with cake and garnish with a sprig of mint.

*Tip:* Keep your butter cold and do not overwork the dough. You can use this recipe with any fruit in season.

# Resources

# Shops and Businesses

## Abundant Acres

Heirloom tomato and pepper plants.

Abundant Acres
P.O. Box 256
Hartville, MO 65667
Phone: (417) 462-1019
Email: abundantacres@yahoo.com
http://www.abundantacres.net

## Baker Creek Heirloom Seed Company

I love these guys. Jere, Emilee, and their daughter, 6-year-old Sasha, are full of life and lots of fun! They work together in their seed business gathering heirloom seeds from around the world. I love buying seeds from them because they have so many.

2278 Baker Creek Road
Mansfield, MO 65704
Phone: 417-924-8917
Email: seeds@rareseeds.com
www.rareseeds.com

## BioLogic Systems, LLC

We had a great time learning from Ian. He has done a lot of research and knows his stuff regarding soil life. Check *Making Vegetables Volume 3* for his interviews. (Biological soil amendments, compost tea products, and more)

9878 Mill Station Road
Sebastopol, CA 95472
Office: (707) 823-2461
Fax: (888) 390-2672
Email: Info@BioLogicSystemsUSA.com
www.BioLogicSystemsUSA.com

## Bountiful Gardens

Heirloom and open pollinated seeds and more.

18001 Shafer Ranch Road
Willits, CA 95490
Phone: (707) 459-6410
Email: bountiful@sonic.net
http://www.bountifulgardens.org
http://www.growbiointensive.org

## Bulk Herb Store

James and I own Bulk Herb Store. I have been working it since I was 13 years old. Now it is our family business. We love working it as a team, learning, and growing together! We carry lots of great books that make a perfect garden library. You can get all the books we mention here. Bulk Herb Store also has a Making Vegetables seed kit, which is a collection of heirloom seeds that range from spring to fall crops. We have the best compost tea brewing mix I have ever used. It is great!

26 West 6th Ave.
Lobelville, TN 37097
Phone:(877)-278-4257
Email:Info@BulkHerbStore.com
www.BulkHerbStore.com

## Deerfield Supplies, LLC

This is a great source for greenhouse and garden supplies; trays, water wand, irrigation, garden fleece (or row cover), polycarbonate greenhouse panels, organic fertilizers, and soil amendments. Mennonite-owned; mail and phone orders only.

2825 Stringtown Road
Elkton, KY 42220
Phone: (270) 265-2425
Fax: (270) 265-2925

## E and R Seeds, LLC

These guys carry a huge selection of heirloom seeds and greenhouse/gardening supplies. Amish-owned; mail or phone orders only.

1356 E 200 S.
Monroe, IN 46772
Phone: (260) 692-6827

## Fedco Seeds

Many heirloom seeds, cold-hardy varieties, and organic growing supplies.

P.O. Box 520
Waterville, ME 04903
Phone: (207) 462-9900
www.fedcoseeds.com

## Johnny's Selected Seeds

More seeds and supplies.

955 Benton Avenue
Winslow, ME 04901
Phone: (877) 564-6697
www.Johnnyseeds.com

## Ohio Earth Food

Another great place for organic fertilizers and soil amendments.

5488 Swamp Street N.E.
Hartville, OH 44632
Phone: (330) 877-9356
Fax: (330) 877-4237
Email: info@ohioearthfood.com
www.ohioearthfood.com

## Peaceful Valley Farm and Garden

Lots of organic growing supplies. Seedling heat mats, potting soil ingredients, grow lights, and much more.

P.O. Box 2209
Grass Valley, CA 95945
Phone: (530) 272-4769
Email: helpdesk@groworganic.com
www.groworganic.com

## Seeds of Diversity Canada

Canadian seed exchange.

P.O. Box 36, Stn Q
Toronto ON M4T 2L7
Phone: (866) 509-7333
Email: mail@seeds.ca
www.seeds.ca

## Seed Savers Exchange

A member-supported seed exchange in Iowa where they are preserving hundreds of rare and endangered varieties. Great source for heirloom seeds.

3094 North Winn Road
Decorah, IA 52101
Phone: (563) 382-5990
Fax: (206) 203-3990
www.seedsavers.org

Massachusetts – (508) 865-6458
Missouri – (314) 994-3900
Tennessee – (800) 397-4153

## T&J Enterprises

A good place to get compost tea mix, along with balanced, organic fertilizer.

Thomas Giannou
2328 W. Providence Ave.
Spokane, WA 99205
Phone: (888) 769-3878
Outside the USA: (509) 327-7670

thomas@tandjenterprises.com
www.tandjenterprises.com

## The Petaluma Seed Bank

Also owned by Jere and Emilee of Baker Creek Seeds.

199 Petaluma Boulevard North
Petaluma, CA 94952
Phone: (707) 509-5171
Email: paul@rareseeds.com
http://rareseeds.com/petaluma-seed-bank/

## Worm's Way

This company carries compost tea supplies, soil amendments, fluorescent lighting, beneficial insects, and much more.

www.wormsway.com
Florida – (813) 621-1792
Indiana – (812) 876-6425
Kentucky – (859) 525-9676

Don't forget to eat your veggies!

# Books to Add to Your Library

*The Heirloom Life Gardener*
by Jere and Emilee Gettle

*Teaming with Microbes*
by Jeff Lowenfels and Wayne Lewis

*Edible Landscaping*
by Rosalind Creasy

*3-Step Vegetable Gardening*
by Steve Mercer and Sally Roth

*The Vegetable Gardener's Bible*
by Edward C. Smith

*Good Bug, Bad Bug*
by Jessica Walliser

*The Intelligent Gardener*
Steve Solomon

*How to Grow More Vegetables*
John Jevens

*Building Soils Naturally*
Phil Nauta

*Seeds of Deception*
Jeffrey Smith

*Tomatoland*
Barry Estabrook

*Making Vegetables Volumes 2 & 3*
Shoshanna Easling

# Index

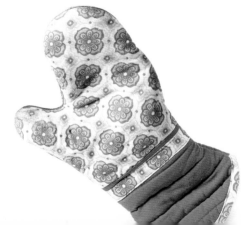

Thank you, Becky Schrock,
Laura Newman, Audrey Madill,
and everyone that was a part of
this project! I am excited to say,
"We did it!"